Medical Law in Finland

Medical Law in Finland

Lasse Lehtonen

This book was originally published as a monograph in the International Encyclopaedia of Laws/Medical Law.

Founding Editor: Roger Blanpain
General Editor: Frank Hendrickx
Volume Editor: Herman Nys; Associate Editor: Tom Goffin

Wolters Kluwer

Published by:
Kluwer Law International B.V.
PO Box 316
2400 AH Alphen aan den Rijn
The Netherlands
E-mail: lrs-sales@wolterskluwer.com
Website: www.wolterskluwer.com/en/solutions/kluwerlawinternational

Sold and distributed by:
Wolters Kluwer Legal & Regulatory U.S.
920 Links Avenue
Landisville, PA 17538
United States of America
E-mail: customer.service@wolterskluwer.com

ISBN 978-94-035-3496-1

e-Book: ISBN 978-94-035-3946-1
web-PDF: ISBN 978-94-035-3956-0

This title is available on www.kluwerlawonline.com

The Author

Lasse Lehtonen works as a professor of health law in the University of Helsinki, Finland. He has the training of both a lawyer and a medical doctor. After graduating from medical school, he got his PhD in immunology in 1989 and was appointed as a senior lecturer in medical microbiology in the University of Turku in 1993. After working several years in pharmaceutical industry, he specialized in clinical pharmacology and was appointed as a senior lecturer in clinical drug research in the University of Helsinki in 1997 and in clinical pharmacology in the University of Tampere in 2004. Prof. Lehtonen also holds a doctorate in law from the University of Helsinki from 2003, where he has worked as a professor of administrative law. He is a senior lecturer in medical law in the University of Lapland and a senior lecturer in administrative law in the University of Turku, Finland. From 2002 onwards, however, Prof. Lehtonen has mainly worked in Helsinki University Hospital, first as the administrative chief physician and now as the director of diagnostic services. In 2011, he was invited for the part-time professorship of health law in the University of Helsinki.

Prof. Lehtonen has authored over 260 publications on immunology, clinical pharmacology, patient safety and on various topics in medical law with special interest in data protection. He has been a member of several advisory bodies on health policies and legislation in Finland. From 2013 to 2022, he was a member of the Expert Panel on Effective Ways of Investing in Health for the European Commission.

The Author

Table of Contents

List of Abbreviations

CNS	Central Nervous System
DNR	Do-Not-Resuscitate
ECHR	European Court of Human Rights
EEA	European Economic Area
EU	European Union
FCCA	Finnish Competition and Consumer Authority
GNP	Gross National Product
HIV	Human Immunodeficiency Virus
IRB	Institutional Review Board
IVF	In Vitro Fertilization
OECD	Organisation for Economic Co-operation and Development
PISA	Programme for International Student Assessment
UN	United Nations

List of Abbreviations

Preface

Finland has during the past twenty years aimed to reform its healthcare system. Finally, in 2021, the social and healthcare reform (sote-reform) was accepted in the Finnish parliament. The new legislation will be applied from 1 January 2023, onwards. The responsibility for arranging services will be transferred from municipalities and hospital districts to new wellbeing service counties. The aim is to integrate healthcare and social care services in all levels and ensure equal access to care in different parts of the country. This volume Medical Law –Finland is one of the first books to comprehensively present the new legislation on the Finnish health system.

Culturally, Finland belongs to Nordic countries with a large political consensus for developing the welfare state according to the Scandinavian model. Public healthcare from the 1960s onwards has been arranged with a Beveridge-type system, where local authorities are responsible for healthcare services that are financed by general taxes. Even though Finland has a relatively high tax rate, a part of the healthcare services has still been financed with national health insurance that is supplementing the system. Furthermore, strong occupational healthcare has ensured access to care for those that are employed. Multiple channels of financing and production have made the Finnish healthcare system complicated and created multiple possibilities for sub-optimization of the care paths. Furthermore, the lack of key professionals (like general practitioners in health centres) in some parts of the system has created bottlenecks for access to care. The sote-reform now tries to make the care paths in public healthcare more feasible for those that need help and care. However, since a large part of the Finnish population belongs to the older age groups that increasingly need services, the economic growth is very slow or even in minus figures and healthcare workforce is insufficient in numbers, there are also many risks for the sote-reform not achieving its goals.

Finland was a forerunner in the world in 1980s to establish a no-fault compensation system for medical damages. The original Act on Patient Damages of 1986 was replaced by the Patient Insurance Act in 2019. However, the criteria for compensation of damages remained essentially the same. The Patient's Rights Act in 1992 was the first specific legislation in the world to codify the general rights of the patient (requirement for good quality care, consent, information and privacy) under one single Act. This Act is still the legal basis for the patients' rights in Finland. Recent developments in medical law in Finland have been greatly overshadowed by issues of the sote-reform. There have, however, been a lot of new regulations concerning electronic health records as well as medical research in Finland. In both areas, the legislation of European Union has impacted greatly the Finnish system, even though Finland has also been a pioneer country in moving from paper records first to regional and then to national data systems and archives that enable the utilization of the patient data in different parts of the care path. At the same time, the requirements for ensuring patient privacy have been increasing. Finland did create specific legislation on biobanks in 2012 and currently, the regulations concerning the utilization of genetic data are under discussion. These new Acts have improved the protection of privacy, but they have, on the other hand, made medical research more complicated and costly, which has created a lot of criticism especially among academic researchers.

Positioning the discipline of medical law within the judicial system and teaching of law has created various solutions in the Finnish universities. Initially, the topic was studied as a part of criminal law, especially when considering the consent issues. Later, issues relating to healthcare services and legal protection of the patients were also studied in the field of administrative law, where the terms 'health law' or 'social law' for the discipline are often used. More recently, medical law has been integrated into a new discipline called 'welfare law', which includes legislation on different types of social benefits. In addition to law students, welfare law courses are now available in faculties of social sciences and to some extent also in medical faculties, especially as a part of specialist education or management courses.

Medical law is a developing discipline that embraces new and interesting questions alongside the social changes in each country. For example, the concept of family in Finland has changed a lot during the past decade, which now creates issues for patient representation. On the other hand, immigration creates cultural conflicts that are sometimes seen also in the healthcare setting. Furthermore, patient's contacts with healthcare providers are becoming more and more digital. All patients are, however, not well-equipped to use the modern digital tools. Finally, the use of big data and more widespread use of genetic data in medical decision making are creating new threats for the autonomy and privacy of the patient. The Medical Law series, with the updated country volumes, make it possible to follow and compare these developments in different countries and find common solutions for the emerging new challenges. I hope that you enjoy reading this volume on the Finnish developments.

General Introduction

§1. General Introduction of the Country

I. Geography

1. The Republic of Finland is one of the north most countries in Europe. In the borders, it has Sweden to the west, Norway to the north, Russia to the east, and Estonia to the south across the Gulf of Finland. By area, it is the eighth largest country in Europe. Baltic Sea forms natural borders to the west and south. However, there are no natural borders to the east and the borders of the country have moved there several times during the turbulences of its history.

2. Due to warm waters of Gulf Stream in North Atlantic, Finland has a milder climate than could be anticipated based on its northern location in the latitudes of Greenland and Alaska. The mean temperature in Helsinki in July is about 17 °C and in January about -6 °C.[1] However, the distance from Helsinki to Utsjoki (the north most village in Finland) is over 1,000 km which is more than from Helsinki to Warsaw and the climate changes considerably, when going inlands from the coastal areas. The mean temperatures in Utsjoki in July are 13 °C and in January about -17 °C.

3. Finland belongs to the northern forest belt (taiga) and 71.6% of the land area is covered with forests. The landscape has been formed by the ice masses of the last ice age that melted some 11,000 years ago, leaving eskers, marshes and almost 190,000 lakes and bonds around the country. Water and forests or forests and snow are the stereotypic representations of Finnish nature for tourists. However, there are huge differences in the landscape, since the north most parts of Finland are above the polar circle and have an arctic climate meaning that the landscape is covered by snow typically about half of the year. The coastal areas, instead, are like anywhere else in the Baltic Sea region except that the see on the coasts of Finland is frozen for one–three months in the winter with exemption of the south most part of the country.

1. Climate Helsinki (Finland), Helsinki climate: Average Temperature, weather by month, Helsinki water temperature – Climate-Data.org, 3 Sep. 2022.

4. Due to the northern climate and short growing period, agriculture is profitable only in the south parts of the country. Therefore, farms in the middle and eastern parts of Finland have mostly grown cattle. Finland is even today – as it has been throughout its history – dependent of the imports of grain and foodstuff to feed its population. The nature has sometimes been very harsh for the people in Finland. One of the last great famines in Europe took place in Finland in 1866–1868 starving some 150,000 –200,000 people (10% of the population) to death.

II. Cultural Compositions

5. Finland was populated shortly after the ice age. The population of gatherer-hunters speaking Finno-Ugric languages (related to Finnish language) arrived to Finland probably some 6,000 years ago. Finland was one of the last countries in Europe to become Christian in the twelfth century and shortly after that the western parts of the modern Finland were rather peacefully joined to the newly established kingdom of Sweden.[2]

6. From the twelfth until the early nineteenth century, Finland was a part of Sweden. The borders of the country were gradually moved eastwards either by immigration or by numerous wars against the neighbouring Russia. Finland ('Eastland') was from the thirteenth century onwards considered as an integral part of the Swedish kingdom with equal rights and obligations as all the other core regions of the country.

7. Sweden was an absolute monarchy from sixteenth to seventeenth century, but after losing its position as the major power in Baltic area to Russia, it started to develop more democratic institutions. The ideas of enlightenment were reflected to the Sweden's eighteenth-century constitution and the legislative powers were vested to the Diet that consisted of four estates (nobleman, clergy, bourgeoisie estate and peasants) even though the monarch grasped more powers in the late eighteenth century. This form of legislative assembly persisted in Finland up to 1906.

8. After Napoleonic wars, Finland was annexed to the Russian Empire. Tsar Alexander I forced Sweden to join Napoleon's Continental system in a war of 1808–1809, but after victory, he granted Finland a status as an autonomous Grand Duchy with its old Swedish laws and legislative system just ousting the Swedish king as the head of state and putting the Czar in that place. This period of autonomy was very important for the development of the national feeling for Finns since the use of Finnish language was actively promoted in the public life by the Russian rulers instead of Swedish language. The last Russian Czar Nicolai I tried in 1899, however, to create more unified Russia and replace the Finnish institutions with the

2. Main outlines of Finnish history, Swedish, Russian and independent eras in a nutshell. Main outlines of Finnish history – thisisFINLAND, 3 Sep. 2022.

authoritarian rule. This created active opposition in Finland and formed the basis for strong Finnish constitutionalism that prevails still today.[3]

9. Finland became independent in 1917 after the Russian Revolution. The declaration of independence was, however, followed by a bitter civil war, when Finnish 'reds' tried to extend the socialist revolution into Finland. Even though the actual hostilities lasted less than four months in spring 1918, the conflict resulted in some 36,000 casualties in a population of 3.1 million people making the Finnish civil war period almost as bloody as the Spanish civil war between 1936 and 1939.[4] However, Finland was able to maintain its democratic system and many social reforms were initiated in 1920s to heal the wounds of the civil war.

10. In the World War II, Finland was first attacked by Stalin's Soviet Union that made a pact with Nazi Germany on the division of Poland, the Baltic countries and Finland. Finland, however, defended herself successfully during the 100-day long winter war in 1939–1940 and was not occupied. When Germany attacked Soviet Union in 1941, Finland joined the attack until it made a separate peace with the Russians in 1944 losing about 15% of its eastern territories as a part of the peace treaty.

11. Finland joined the United Nations (UN) in 1955 and established an official policy of neutrality but took in the 1960s and 1970s carefully into consideration the security interests of the neighbour superpower. Nevertheless, it remained active on the world stage emphasizing the role of UN in global security. Accordingly, Finland has been very active in UN mandated peace keeping mission.

12. After the collapse of Soviet Union, Finland joined European Union (EU) in 1995, but did not yet join any military alliances. After the Russian invasion to Ukraine in February 2022, however, Finland together with Sweden applied for membership in North Atlantic Treaty Organization. Finland maintains its own defence forces with a large conscription army and relatively big defence budget (about 2% of the GNP).[5]

III. Political System

13. Finland is a parliamentary republic with a central government based in the capital of Helsinki, local governments in 309 municipalities and an autonomous region, the Åland Islands, where Swedish is the only official language. The autonomy of Åland and its demilitarization are based on international conventions

3. Lavapuro J, Ojanen T & Scheinin M, Rights-Based Constitutionalism in Finland and the Development of Pluralist Constitutional Review, International Journal of Constitutional Law, Volume 9, Issue 2, April 2011, pp. 505–531. https://academic.oup.com/icon/article/9/2/505/649575, 3 Sep. 2022.
4. Kekkonen J, Kun Aseet Puhuvat. Art House 2016.
5. Ministry of Defence: Puolustusministeriön hallinnonalan osuus BKT.stä, BKTosuus.pdf (defmin.fi), 3 Sep. 2022.

originating from Crimean war peace treaty of 1856 and from the 1921 decision of the League of Nations to the dispute between Finland and Sweden.[6]

14. Finland's republican constitution combines a parliamentary system with a relatively strong presidency. Legislative powers are vested in the Eduskunta (parliament), a unicameral body established in 1906. Members of parliament are elected for four-year terms by proportional representation from fifteen multi-member electoral districts under universal suffrage at age 18. Finland was the first country in Europe to grant suffrage to women in national elections (1906).[7] The four most popular parties in the general elections of 2019 were the Social Democrats (Suomen Sosiaalidemokraattinen Puolue), the nationalist True Finns (Perussuomalaiset), Conservatives (Kokoomus) and the Centre Party (Keskusta). Due to fragmented political field, a coalition of the parties is needed for the majority government. The voting turnout in general elections has been around 70%.

15. National referendums, which are consultative, have been used twice: in 1931, on the ending of the prohibition of alcohol, and in 1994, on EU membership, when 57% of the voters supported the membership.

16. Finland's political system traditionally has been more like the French than most other European parliamentary democracies because of the division of executive powers between the president and the cabinet led by the Prime Minister. On 1 March 2000, a new Finnish constitution entered into force.[8] The new constitution increases the power of the parliament in relation to the Cabinet (Valtioneuvosto) and increases the power of the Cabinet in relation to the president.

17. The President of the Republic is the formal Head of State in Finland. The President is the leader of foreign policy, and the commander-in-chief of the Finnish defence forces. He/she is directly elected by absolute majority for a six-year term, renewable once. The President appoints the Prime Minister based on the suggestion of the chairman of the parliament. Before the constitutional reform in 2000, the President enjoyed even more powers (e.g., having the power to dissolve the parliament for new elections). Now the main executive power, however, lies in the Cabinet which is appointed and headed by the Prime Minister who is responsible only to the parliament and has the right to ask premature elections from the President in the case of political deadlock.

18. Since 1995 Finland is a member of EU currently with fourteen seats in the European Parliament.

---

6. Finnish Government: Centenary celebrations of the autonomy of the Åland Islands set to begin, Centenary celebrations of the autonomy of the Åland Islands set to begin (valtioneuvosto.fi), 3 Sep. 2022.
7. Nations Encyclopedia: Finland –Government, https://www.nationsencyclopedia.com/Europe/Finland-GOVERNMENT.html#ixzz6zJN8sQTc, 3 Sep. 2022.
8. Parliament of Finland: The Constitution of Finland and Parliament's Rules of Procedure, Publication by the Parliamentary Office 3/2013, https://www.eduskunta.fi/FI/naineduskuntatoimii/julkaisut/Documents/ekj_3+2013.pdf, 3 Sep. 2022.

19. The local government in municipalities has had a strong position in Finland. This is due both to the Scandinavian tradition of 'things' that were organized also in Finland and to the long distances and poor transports until the twentieth century that have made it difficult for the central government to keep contacts to the different parts of the country. In the Middle Ages, things were the public assemblies of the freemen of a region.[9] They functioned as both parliaments and courts solving disputes and making political decisions.

20. The modern Finnish municipalities have council-manager government. The council (*kunnanvaltuusto*) is elected for a four-year term and answers only to the voters. The size of the council is proportional to the population. A subsection of the council, the municipal executive board (*kunnanhallitus*), controls the municipal government and monitors the implementation of decisions of the council. Its decisions must be approved by the council. Unlike national cabinets, its composition is derived from the composition of the council, not along government-opposition lines. Furthermore, individual decisions are prepared in specialized municipal boards (*lautakunta*) for a council meeting, which include, for example, zoning, social assistance, and education boards. Council, executive board, and municipal board memberships are elected positions of responsibility, not full-time jobs. The municipalities have the right to tax their inhabitants, but part of their income is also derived from the state. The central government is subsidizing those tasks (like healthcare and primary education) that the municipalities are legally bound to carry out. However, the social and healthcare reform of 2021 is moving healthcare and social care from municipalities to newly established counties.

21. As a result of the social and healthcare reform of 2021, Finland will have twenty-one wellbeing services counties and City of Helsinki that are responsible for healthcare and social care and will get their full funding from the state.[10] The counties will have their own council and executive board, but they will not (yet) have the right to collect taxes from the inhabitants. The first county councils were elected in January 2022 for their four-year term.

22. Judicial powers in Finland belong to independent courts. The Finnish Constitution guarantees everyone the right to have his case heard appropriately and without undue delay by a court or other public authority. Everyone also has the right to have a decision affecting his rights and duties reviewed by a court or other judicial body. The Finnish court system is divided into two categories. Firstly, general courts that deal with civil and criminal matters. Secondly, administrative courts that deal with disputes between a public authority and private individuals. The highest judicial instances are the Supreme Court and the Supreme Administrative Court.

9. Ahlness EA: Vikings in World History the Legacy of the Ting: Viking Justice, Egalitarianism, and Modern Scandinavian Regional Governance, Forum: Vikings in World History, 2020, https://www.researchgate.net/publication/340661469_Vikings_in_World_History_The_Legacy_of_the_Ting_Viking_Justice_Egalitarianism_and_Modern_Scandinavian_Regional_Governance, 3 Sep. 2020.
10. Sote-uudistus: New structure, https://soteuudistus.fi/en/new-structure, 3 Sep. 2022.

These courts, if they are in doubt about the interpretation or validity of an EU law, should ask the Court of Justice of EU for clarification.

23. Finland is also a member of the Council of Europe and the decisions of the European Court of Human Rights are well-respected in the Finnish judicial system.

IV. Population and Vital Statistics

24. Finland's population in 2021 was just above 5.5 million, with the majority concentrated in its southern regions.[11] About 1 million residents live in the Helsinki capital area, which also produces about one-third of the country's GDP.

25. As in other European countries, the birth rate in Finland has been declining steadily during the past decades. The birth rate in 1990 was 1.78 per woman while it was only 1.37 in 2020. The low birth rate suggests that the population in Finland will start to decrease after 2035 without significant immigration. Immigration to Finland has, however, been less active than e.g., to Sweden. Currently, some 8% of the Finnish population have a foreign background. Some 5% of the people living in Finland had another than Finnish citizenship in 2020.[12] The biggest immigration to Finland has come from Russia (or former Soviet Union) and Estonia.

26. At present, the post-war baby boomer generation (1945–1950) is getting to old age and the aging population is putting pressures on Finnish economy and welfare system. The economic maintenance ratio between people that are working and those that have retired or are outside the labour market in Finland is currently above 130% meaning that for every working people there are over 1.3 people that are not working.[13] The population-based maintenance ratio (e.g., people below 15 or above 65 in relation to the working age people) is currently 0.62 but will increase to 0.66 by 2030.[14]

27. The life expectancy in Finland is of good European standard. As a matter of fact, the life expectancy of 85 years for Finnish females in 2020 is the highest in EU.[15] Unfortunately, Finnish males are not surviving as long, since their life expectancy is 79 years, putting the life expectancy of the whole population to 82 years.

11. Statistics Finland: Population and Society, Population and Society | Statistics Finland (tilastokeskus.fi), 3 Sep. 2022.
12. Statistics Finland: Foreign citizens, Foreign citizens | Statistics Finland (tilastokeskus.fi), 3 Sep. 2022.
13. Statistics Finland: Economic dependency ratio was 132 in 2018, Statistics Finland – 1. Economic dependency ratio was 132 in 2018, 3 Sep. 2022.
14. Statistics Finland: Number of young people in danger of diminishing considerably due to the decrease in birth rate, Statistics Finland – Population projection 2018–2070, 3 Sep. 2022.
15. Eurostat: Mortality and life expectancy statistics. Mortality and life expectancy statistics – Statistics Explained (europa.eu), 3 Sep. 2022.

Furthermore, Finland is among the ten safest countries in the world to be born since the infant mortality rate is only just above two deaths for 1,000 new-borns.[16]

28. The most common causes of death in Finland are cardiovascular diseases (34%) and cancer (25%). Coronary heart disease that used to kill Finns in big numbers has decreased dramatically in the past 30 years due to active public health measures.[17] Finland also used to have a high incidence of suicides (comparable to Japan), but their number has dropped dramatically during the past 20 years.[18]

29. Finland was a largely agrarian country until the 1950s. Thereafter, it rapidly developed an advanced economy while building an extensive Nordic-style welfare state. Forest industry (timber, pulp, and paper) was the main form of manufacturing up to 1980s but was thereafter replaced by telecommunication and machinery.

30. Today, Finland has a highly industrialized mixed economy and the whole economy depends greatly on exports. The Gross National Product (GNP) per capita in 2021 was about USD 53,900, which is, however, lower than in other Nordic countries due to the stagnating economy after the euro crisis in 2010.[19] The largest sector of the economy is services at 69%, followed by manufacturing and refining at 28%. Finland, unlike the other Nordic countries, joined the Eurozone already at its inception in 1999.

V. Social and Cultural Values

31. Culturally, Finland belongs to the family of Nordic countries (Sweden, Finland, Denmark, Norway, and Iceland having together some 27 million inhabitants). The Nordic societal model typically has a high degree of income redistribution (with progressive taxation) and little social unrest due to various free welfare services. The Nordic model of welfare state is widely accepted in Finland and there are no big differences between political parties in relation to the welfare state, even though the amount of public spending is causing political debate across the traditional right – left line. However, since political coalitions are a necessity to form a government in Finland, the political culture is very keen on making compromises and even differences on budget policies are often set a side, when governments include both left and right-wing parties.

16. World Health Organization: Finland, Finland (who.int), 3 Sep. 2022.
17. Jousilahti P, Laatikainen T, Salomaa V et al: 40-Year CHD Mortality Trends and the Role of Risk Factors in Mortality Decline: The North Karelia Project Experience, Glob Heart 2016:207,207–212.
18. National institute for health and welfare: Decline in the number of suicides has stopped in Finland – new means are needed to achieve WHO's goal, Decline in the number of suicides has stopped in Finland – new means are needed to achieve WHO's goal – News – THL 4 Sep. 2022.
19. The World Bank: GDP per capita (current US$), GDP per capita (current US$) – Finland | Data (worldbank.org), 4 Sep. 2022.

32. Finns themselves consider their country to be culturally very homogenous. However, the country's position between east and west has left an impact on the culture and population that Finns do not consider self very divisive, but which demonstrates a lot of multiculturalism and tolerance.

33. The Swedish legacy in Finnish history is reflected in the prevalence of the Swedish language in Finland and its official status as the second national language. Nowadays, only 5% of the population have Swedish as their native language and English has largely replaced Swedish even in the Nordic co-operation. In late nineteenth century, there were some disputes between the language groups, when the position of the Finnish language in the society was improving rapidly. Many families changed their Swedish names to Finnish ones to reflect the nationalistic feelings. Language disputes largely disappeared after the independence of the country. Since the number of Swedish speaking is constantly diminishing, there is some new discussion, whether bilingual services are too costly for the country. Accordingly, Swedish language is not any more obligatory for Finnish students.

34. Sweden was turned protestant in the sixteenth century by the command of King Gustav Wasa, which order was loyally followed also in Finland. There have never been any internal religious conflicts within Finland. Some 68% of the Finnish population nowadays belong to Evangelical Lutheran church and about 1% to the Greek Orthodox Church. The position of the Greek Orthodox Church is partly due to the fact that Finns were baptized from both east and west in the Middle Ages and partly due to the influence of the Russian Czars in the nineteenth century, who wanted to support the Greek Orthodox Church in Finland. These two churches are still official state religions, even though the country is very secularized. Catholic Church is very small in Finland having only some 15,000 members.

35. Finland has had an Islamic congregation already from the late nineteenth century onwards (oldest in any of the Nordic countries) due to the immigration of so-called Tatars from Russia (mainly form the area of Nižni Novgorod) to Helsinki area either as part of the imperial Russian army or as merchants.[20] The number of Muslims has, however, increased considerably during the past 20 years due to immigration especially from Somalia and Iraq. The estimate of the number of Muslims in 2020 is around 50,000 even though their number is increasing. Discussion on immigration has in Finland, as in other European countries, increased the popularity of nationalistic movements. However, the social problems caused by immigration have been much less pronounced in Finland than e.g., in Sweden. Finland has also a small Jewish congregation. As the Tatars, also the Finnish Jews mostly came from Russia during the imperial period in the nineteenth century. There has been little or no antisemitism in Finland.[21]

---

20. The Nomad Today: Finnish Tatars, two centuries of Muslim faith shaped by ice and snow, Finnish Tatars, two centuries of Muslim faith shaped by ice and snow (thenomadtoday.com), 4 Sep. 2022.
21. European Union Agency for Fundamental Rights: Antisemitism: Overview of antisemitic incidents recorded in the European Union 2009-2019, https://fra.europa.eu/en/publication/2020/antisemitism-overview-2009-2019, 4 Sep. 2022.

36. One feature of the cultural heritage in Finland is the heavy emphasis on public education. The Protestant church required from the seventeenth century onwards that before confirmation (and confirmation was a prerequisite for marriage) one should be able to read and write. This rule applied both to males and females. Already in 1880s some 98% of the Finnish population was fully literate and Finland is now on the top ranks in international studies comparing the literacy rate.[22] Finland has also scored top rankings in the Organisation for Economic Co-operation and Development's (OECD) Programme for International Student Assessment (PISA) that measures 15-year-olds' ability to use their reading, mathematics and science knowledge and skills to meet real-life challenges.[23] Finnish Universities, however, are behind their Nordic counterparts in the international rankings. Both basic and higher education is free in Finland.

37. Gender equality is regarded as a fundamental human right and a core value in Finland.[24] About 75% of the Finnish women between 20 and 64 years of age are working, which is just little bit less than about 78% for men and well above the EU average of 67%.[25] The salary level for females in 2019 was, however, only 84% of the salary levels of males. Income differences in Finland are still rather small and they are further balanced by progressive taxation.[26]

38. The Finnish society is in general described by homogeneity and social coherence. Finland is one of the most stable countries in the world. In 2022, Finland was also named the happiest place in the world for a fifth year running in the annual UN-sponsored report.[27]

39. Although the World Happiness Reports are based on a wide variety of data, the most important source to evaluate happiness in a country is the Gallup World Poll,[28] which is unique in the range and comparability of its global series of annual surveys. Finland in 2022 once again took the top spot as the happiest country in the world according to survey data. It has ranked very high on the measures of mutual trust that have helped to protect lives and livelihoods even during the coronavirus pandemic. Based on different international surveys, it is very clear that the Nordic model of welfare state with the good education level of the Finnish people is maintaining the culture of trust to the democratic government in Finland. This trust for

22. The Guardian: Finland ranked world's most literate country, Finland ranked world's most literate nation | Books | The Guardian, 4 Sep. 2022.
23. OECD: What is PISA, https://www.oecd.org/pisa/, 4 Sep. 2022.
24. Ministry of Social Affairs and Health: Gender equality in Finland, https://stm.fi/documents/1271139/5825735/sukupuolten_tasa_arvo_suomessa_UK_verkko_V1.pdf/7464741f-29b4-4acc-b01e-718449d55b01/sukupuolten_tasa_arvo_suomessa_UK_verkko_V1.pdf, 4 Sep. 2022.
25. Eurostat: Women's employment in the EU, https://ec.europa.eu/eurostat/web/products-eurostat-news/-/edn-20200306-1, 4 Sep. 2022.
26. The Union of Journalists in Finland: Income equality in Finland among the best in Europe, https://journalistiliitto.fi/en/income-equality-in-finland-among-the-best-in-europe/, 4 Sep. 2022.
27. World Happiness Report: Read the Report, World Happiness Report 2022 | The World Happiness Report, 4 Sep. 2022.
28. Gallup: Understanding the Thoughts, Feelings and Behaviours of People Around the World, https://www.gallup.com/analytics/318875/global-research.aspx, 4 Sep. 2022.

the government and legislative process as the way to improve the wellbeing of people is also important for organization of healthcare in Finland.

§2. General Description of the Healthcare System

I. Administration of the Healthcare System in Finland

40. The Ministry of Social Affairs and Health has the formal leadership for public healthcare in Finland. It has the task to promote good health and functional capacity of people and to secure sufficient health and social services. The ministry has tried to gain more steering power in the sote-reform, even though the actual healthcare services are produced by self-governing municipalities and in the future counties.

41. The Ministry has several central agencies under its leadership, whose activities it coordinates. The National Institute for Health and Welfare (THL) studies, monitors, and develops measures to promote the wellbeing and health of the population in Finland.[29] Its functions also include several specialist tasks e.g., in the field of prevention of infectious disease. The other central agency, the National Supervisory Authority for Welfare and Health (Valvira) guides, supervises and runs the licensing administration of social and healthcare.[30]

42. The third central agency, the Finnish Medicines Agency (Fimea) is responsible for licensing and supervisory tasks related to pharmaceuticals, medical devices and pharmacies.[31]

43. Regional State Administrative Agencies are part of the civil service. They are responsible for supervising healthcare services on the regional level. These agencies, in collaboration with Valvira, also supervise healthcare professionals.

29. The National Institute for Health and Welfare: What is THL, What is THL? – THL, 5 Sep. 2022.
30. Valvira: Valvira – promoting health and welfare through effective supervision, Valvira – Front page – valvira englanti, 5 Sep. 2022.
31. Fimea: Organisation, Organisation–fimea englanti–Fimea, 5 Sep. 2022.

Figure 1 Administration of Social and Healthcare in Finland[32]

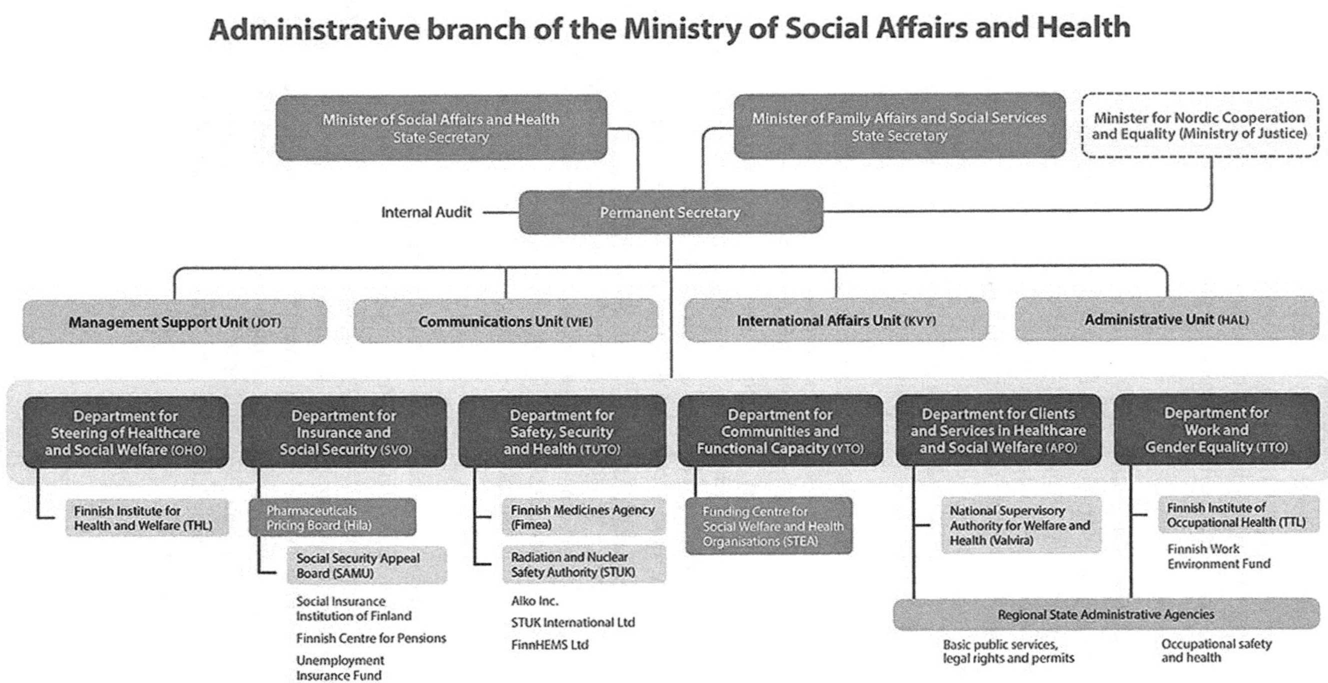

32. Ministry of Social Affairs and Health: Administrative branch, Administrative branch–Ministry of Social Affairs and Health (stm.fi), 5 Sep. 2022.

44. Finnish administrative system follows strong legalistic tradition.[33] It has its origins from late nineteenth century when the autonomy of the Finnish Grand Duchy was defended against the Czars efforts to unify it with Russia. Unlike Sweden, Norway or Denmark, the form of government in Finland after independence was chosen to be republic with rather strong position of the President of the Republic.

45. The original constitution of 1919 did not have any mention on social rights. In the constitutional reform of 1995, the status of basic human rights in the constitution was strengthened. In addition to classical civil rights, also social rights were included into the list of basic human rights. The aim was to make all basic rights legally binding. This means that good health of the people in Finland is not just an important societal goal, but everybody in Finland has the right to adequate healthcare services.[34] The reformed section of basic rights was taken as such to the second chapter of the new Finnish constitution in 2000.

46. Section 19 of the Finnish constitution states that the public authorities shall guarantee for everyone, as provided in more detail by an Act, adequate social, health and medical services and promote the health of the population. Section 6 of the constitution ensures the equality of people. These two sections have been the basis for the Finnish healthcare reform that has been planned from the first years of this millennium. Since healthcare has been organized by municipalities, there have been differences in the level of services in different parts of the country.[35] This was seen as a major problem for the equality of the Finnish people. Furthermore, the adequacy of healthcare services in section 19 means that public authorities should make it possible for everybody to participate in the functions of society as a competent member. This requires in practice that the public bodies arranging healthcare should have sufficient resources at their disposal to be able to carry out their legal obligations.

47. There has been a general consensus that most municipalities in Finland are too small and have inadequate resources to be able to take care of their obligations in healthcare and social care. However, section 121 of the Finnish constitution also guarantees the self-government of the residents in the municipalities. Unlike in Sweden, Finland has not had a middle-level public authority whose members would be selected in elections. The regional administration has, instead, been an extension of the central government with authority to make administrative decisions or to supervise the municipalities. However, the healthcare reform of 2021 is now changing the system radically.

33. Mäenpää, Olli: Hallinto-oikeus. Helsinki 2013.
34. Tuori K, Kotkas T: Sosiaalioikeus. Helsinki 2016.
35. Arajärvi P: Johdatus sosiaalioikeuteen. Helsinki 2011.

II. Healthcare Spending in Finland

48. Health spending per capita in Finland has increased at a moderate rate over the past 10 years. Before COVID pandemic, the health spending accounted for 9.2% of Finland's GDP, which is lower than both the EU average (9.9%) and the share in Denmark, Sweden and Norway (all above 10%).[36] Public funding accounts for 77% of all health spending, a lower share than the EU average (80%). Most of the remaining expenses are paid out of pocket by households.[37]

49. In 2019, Finland spent EUR 3,135 per person on health (adjusted for differences in purchasing power), less than the EU average (EUR 3,521) and substantially less than Denmark, Sweden and Norway. In terms of public spending priorities, the share of government spending allocated to health is also lower in Finland than in the EU as a whole and in other Nordic countries, at 13% in 2017 compared to 16% (EU average and Denmark) and 18% (Sweden and Norway).

50. Some 77% of health spending is financed through public sources (compared to an EU average of 80%), with the remaining 23% paid by private sources (higher than the 14%–17% share in other Nordic countries and the 20% EU average). Most of this private expenditure comes from out-of-pocket (OOP) payments, of which outpatient medical care, dental care, pharmaceuticals and long-term care account for the majority. Private insurance has increased its role in health financing, even though its share in 2019 was only 2% of total health spending.

51. User fees are extensive and involve the majority of services, including primary and emergency care. Two forms of protection from excessive user fees are in place: caps on annual payments and exemptions. There are separate annual caps in 2022 on services (EUR 692), prescribed outpatient medicines (EUR 59,212) and transportation costs (EUR 300). Medicines included in the reimbursement list are reimbursed at 40%, 65% or 100%, depending largely on the severity of the condition. Exemptions involve specific services (e.g., treatment of certain infectious diseases, immunizations, maternity and child health clinics, provision of medical aids), and most services are free for children under 18. However, this type of health coverage design, with substantial out-of-pocket spending and unequal distribution of available services across municipalities/counties, raises concerns about barriers to accessing health services.

52. More than two-thirds of Finnish people report being in good health, a share similar to the EU as a whole. However, people on lower incomes are considerably less likely to report being in good health: less than 60% in the lowest income group report being in good health, compared to over 80% in the highest. This difference

36. European Observatory on Health Systems and Policies: Finland: Country Health Profile 2021, Finland: Country Health Profile 2021 (who.int), 9 Sep. 2022.
37. Eurostat: Current healthcare expenditure, analysed by source of financing 2019, File:Current healthcare expenditure, analysed by source of financing, 2019 (% of current healthcare expenditure).png–Statistics Explained (europa.eu), 9 Sep. 2022.

is greater than in other Nordic countries or the EU average. Although it has decreased, the gender gap in life expectancy remains large and above the EU average. Inequalities in life expectancy in Finland exist not only by gender but also by socioeconomic status. In 2017, life expectancy for men at age 30 with the lowest level of education was about 5.1 years lower than for the most educated. This education gap in longevity was smaller among women, at 3.6 years. The gap between the least and most educated women increased during the last decade, while it narrowed slightly for men. Many behavioural risk factors in Finland are more common among people with lower education or income. In 2017-2018, one in six adults (18%) who had not completed secondary education smoked daily, compared to only one in sixteen (6%) among those with tertiary education. In the same vein, 24% of people without secondary education were defined as obese, compared to only 17% among those with higher education. This higher prevalence of risk factors among socially disadvantaged groups contributes significantly to inequalities in health and life expectancy.[38]

III. The Long-Way to the Healthcare Reform of 2021

53. Congregations and municipalities formed the local administration in Finland in the nineteenth century.[39] After the great famine of 1866–1868, it was evident that better protection from hunger and disease was needed for the growing population of Finland. The Imperial Healthcare Act for the Grand Duchy of Finland from 1879 made it obligatory for municipalities to provide healthcare and maintenance for the sick and disabled.[40] Doctors were, however, few in the country: in 1910, there were just totally 159 doctors in the municipalities. Hospitals were run by the state and they were few and poorly equipped. Those who could afford travelled often to Sweden, Germany or Switzerland for treatment.

54. From the 1930s, the municipalities started to build their own hospitals, as well to make the specialized care available for their inhabitants. Those hospitals were either run by an individual city or by an alliance of municipalities in rural areas. In addition, a network of tuberculosis hospitals was established in the 1930s and 1940s. Up to the 1950s, there was only one medical faculty in Finland in the University of Helsinki and many Finnish physicians were trained abroad.

55. In the 1960s, there were two competing political approaches for financing healthcare in Finland. One was based on insurance model (Bismarck model) and the other one on tax-based public health services (Beveridge model). Finland established national health insurance as late as in 1964 to compensate healthcare costs.

38. Terveyden ja hyvinvoinnin laitos: Kansallinen terveys–, hyvinvointi– ja palvelututkimus Finsote, Tulosraportti maakunnat 2017–2018 – Kansallinen terveys–, hyvinvointi- ja palvelututkimus FinSote – THL (terveytemme.fi), 9 Sep. 2022.
39. Forsius A: Vuoden 1879 terveydenhoitosääntö. Suomen Lääkärilehti 1989:25,2508.
40. Forsius A: Suomen terveydenhuollon murros 1880-luvulla, Suomen terveydenhuollon murros 1880-luvulla (saunalahti.fi), 10 Sep. 2022.

However, in 1972, the new public health legislation also established a Beveridge-type system in Finland. The Public Health Act (66/1972) required that municipalities establish local health centres with multitude of services from maternity clinics to rehabilitation. This system was rather disintegrated even though the Ministry of Social Affairs and Health had the formal leadership on the system and a central agency (National Board of Health) supervised the local authorities. The self-governing municipalities could, however, in practice develop their services as they saw fit. The health insurance system prevailed in parallel of the public service and provided especially those services that were not easily available from the local health centres (like dentistry and ophthalmology).

56. Finnish public healthcare system was truly formed only in the 1960s and 1970s as part of the building of the welfare state mainly following the Swedish model. The Finnish system, however, was based on the municipalities (instead of counties) that had to organize the healthcare for their inhabitants. Municipalities in Finland have the right to tax inhabitants and businesses in their area giving them assets to invest in any societal functions their councils find necessary.

57. The public health legislation in the 1970s in Finland turned the tide in excessive premature mortality. Especially the Finnish success in reducing cardiovascular risk factors and cardiovascular mortality received even international appreciation.[41] Finland has been very successful also in the screening programmes for cancer, diminishing smoking and in prevention of traffic accidents.

58. General legislation for hospital services was accepted only in 1989 (Act of Specialized Healthcare 1062/1989). Municipalities were then required to join one of the twenty hospital districts (sairaanhoitopiiri) that were responsible for hospital services. In addition, Åland Islands were allowed to arrange their healthcare services within their self-governance. By 1980s, Finland had five medical faculties (Helsinki, Turku, Tampere, Kuopio and Oulu) that were combined with modern university hospitals. Even though the number of hospital districts (twenty) was pretty high for a country of just over 5 million people, there were also so-called specific responsibility areas (erityisvastuualueet) for each university hospital in which the more specialized care was arranged and coordinated with the local hospitals.

59. Discussion on the need of a healthcare reform started in the end of 1990s. Finland had in the early 1990s a major economic depression due to the collapse of Soviet trade, unsuccessful currency policies and a bank crisis. From the beginning, the reform was linked with the role and number of municipalities in Finland. In 1999, there were totally 459 municipalities in Finland many of which were very small and unable alone to organize social and healthcare services. In 2021, there are still 309 municipalities in Finland indicating that about one-third of the municipalities have merged with another municipality. Their size varies about thousandfold

41. The National Institute for Health and Welfare: The North Karelia Project fundamentally changed the lifestyle of Finns and increased healthy years of life, The North Karelia Project fundamentally changed the lifestyle of Finns and increased healthy years of life – News –THL, 10 Sep. 2022.

from 699 inhabitants (Luhanka) to 656920 inhabitants (Helsinki). The Finnish constitution (section 121) guarantees that the municipalities have the right to self-governance which had also made it difficult to change their role in healthcare without their voluntary contribution.

60. The first efforts to reform the healthcare were made in 2003 during the prime ministership of Paavo Lipponen. The aim of the 'national health project' was to improve the coordination between different players, especially between hospitals. The project emphasized the need to centralize the treatment of some patient groups and tried to reduce the number of 24/7 emergency rooms that were scattered often to small hospitals in Finland.

61. The next two suggestions for the reform in 2007 and 2011 were characterized by the efforts to primarily reform the role of municipalities. In 2007, the reform by the cabinet of prime minister Matti Vanhanen aimed to form bigger municipalities with about 20,000 people that would better be able to arrange services for their inhabitants. However, this aim was only partly achieved and the number of municipalities in Finland in 2011 was about 330.[42]

62. In 2011, the cabinet of Jyrki Katainen put more emphasis to reform social and healthcare. His cabinet suggested that instead of merging municipalities, the central cities in a region would carry the main responsibility for the arrangement of services for the whole region. This idea was, however, found unconstitutional in the Finnish parliament, since the reform would have put people living in different municipalities to an unequal position. There was, however, a separate effort in the parliament to arrange all social and healthcare services in hospital districts that are formed by all municipalities in the region. However, since their boards and councils are not elected by popular vote, this would have created problems for the democratic supervision of the districts, which would have had most of the income of the local taxes in their possession.

63. In 2015, the cabinet of Juha Sipilä tried to combine the public and private healthcare in his model for the social and healthcare reform. His cabinet suggested that healthcare and social services would be arranged by counties instead on municipalities. However, the patients should have had the opportunity to select a private healthcare provider instead of a public health centre or hospital. This suggestion was again doomed as unconstitutional in the parliament, since it aimed also to reduce healthcare costs without confirming the necessary level of services that are protected by section 19 of the Finnish constitution.

64. Finally, in 2020, the cabinet of Prime Minister Sanna Marin made their proposal for the reform. It kept the idea of moving social and healthcare services from municipalities to larger areas (now called counties), but dropped the idea of including private providers as an alternative to public services. Collecting all the services

42. Koski A, Kyösti A, Halonen J: Kuntaliitokset suurennuslasin alla, https://vm.fi/documents/10623/307637/Kuntaliitokset+suurennuslasin+alla/58c9b7d5-f34d-47d6-9e49-66653b00c904, 10 Sep. 2022.

into the counties will make the integration of primary healthcare and hospital services as well as combining healthcare and social services possible. Her cabinet is also trying to abolish the national health insurance as a source of funding for visits to doctors or dentists. However, also pharmaceuticals are reimbursed from the national health insurance making the total termination of the national health insurance system in Finland very difficult.

IV. The Sote-Reform of 2021

65. In June 2021, the social and healthcare reform (sote) was approved in the Finnish parliament.[43] The relevant acts will enter into force in stages, the first ones on 1 July 2021 and the last ones on 1 January 2023. The Act on Organizing Healthcare and Social Welfare Services (612/2021) lays down provisions on the responsibility for organizing healthcare and social welfare, the promotion of health and wellbeing, the securing of locally accessible services and linguistic rights, and the guidance, direction and supervision of wellbeing services counties. The reform is based on strong public sector and reliance on the Beveridge-type system. However, the model also includes a lot of elements of planned economy in contrast to previous suggestions to have a more patient-oriented approach for healthcare.

66. Altogether twenty-one wellbeing services counties will be established in Finland and entrusted with the health, social and rescue services duties that are currently the responsibility of municipalities and joint municipal authorities.[44] Furthermore, the City of Helsinki will still be responsible for organizing healthcare, social welfare and rescue services. The responsibility for health, social and rescue services duties will therefore rest with totally twenty-two organizers. In addition, the joint county authority for the Hospital District of Helsinki and Uusimaa (Helsinki University Hospital) will have a special status and it will be responsible for organizing specialized healthcare in Uusimaa area.

67. All healthcare and social welfare personnel and their tasks will be transferred from municipalities and joint municipal authorities to the wellbeing service counties. Personnel will be transferred also from the joint municipal support services to the employment of the wellbeing services counties, if at least half of their present duties were devoted to municipal health, social or rescue services. In the beginning of 2023, about 172,900 people currently employed by 332 municipalities or joint municipal authorities will be transferred to the employment of the wellbeing services counties in line with the transfer-of-business principle.

---

43. Sote-uudistus: Health and social services reform, Government proposal for health and social services reform and related legislation adopted by Parliament – (soteuudistus.fi) 10 Sep. 2022.
44. Niemivuo, Matti: Uusi aluehallinto – hyvinvointialueista maakuntaitsehallintoon? Kauppakamari 2022.

68. The operation of hospital districts and special care districts will be transferred to the counties, as well. The wellbeing services counties and the municipalities will both be responsible for promoting health and wellbeing. The municipalities will retain the responsibility for the organization of environmental healthcare. However, subject to certain conditions, municipalities and counties can agree to organize environmental healthcare duties as part of healthcare and social welfare services.

69. A county council, elected by direct popular vote, will be the highest decision-making body of each wellbeing services county. The first elections were held on 23 January 2022. The activities of each wellbeing services counties will be managed in accordance with the strategy for the counties approved by the council, which will also decide on the organizational structure of the county.

70. The Ministry of Social Affairs and Health will confirm the strategic objectives of healthcare, social welfare and rescue services every four years. The wellbeing services counties must take the objectives into account in their own activities and when preparing agreements on the organization of collaborative areas for healthcare and social welfare. An advisory board for healthcare and social welfare will be established under the Ministry of Social Affairs and Health. The Cabinet will appoint the board for a term of four years. Its task will be to monitor and assess the fulfilment of health and social services duties and support the national guidance and direction of healthcare and social welfare.

71. For the part of demanding specialized medical care, Finland has been divided into five co-operation areas according to the university hospitals coverage of the counties. The activities which require the most demanding specialized knowledge have been centralized to university hospitals. The counties in the co-operation area have together to take care of the guidance and consulting that is required for the proper division of tasks.

72. The distribution of tasks between hospitals must promote quality, patient safety, effectiveness and productivity of healthcare. The counties must also agree on the organizing of the areal emergency care centre. The co-operation must cover data system decisions, medical rehabilitation and procurements. In order to match these, the counties within the co-operation area must make a co-operation agreement as required in section 43 of Healthcare Act. The division of tasks of specialized medical care must be agreed on the level of the co-operation area. In addition, the agreement must include a common process on the implementation of new healthcare practices. The council of the counties must approve the co-operation agreement of specialized medical care. If they cannot reach an agreement, the State Council (i.e., the Cabinet) can decide the contents of the agreement.

73. Specialized medical care can also nationally be centralized into one co-operation area, if the centralization or the treatment is appropriate. The Cabinet gives out a specific decree on treatments that should be centralized either regionally or nationally.[45]

V. Financing of the Healthcare System

74. The activities of the wellbeing services counties will be funded mainly by central government and partly from client fees to be collected from the users of services. Provisions on funding will be laid in the Act on the Funding of the Wellbeing Services Counties (617/2021). The funding of wellbeing services counties will be universal. It will be divided among the counties based on imputed factors related to service needs and circumstances, covering healthcare and social welfare and rescue services. Some of the funding will be based on population numbers and some will be determined by the criteria for health and wellbeing performance.

75. The imputed funding for healthcare and social welfare will be based on the service need coefficients that describe the need for healthcare, social welfare and services for older people. In calculating these coefficients, account will be taken of the information on the age and gender structure, morbidity and socio-economic factors of the population and their use of services as well as the costs arising from the use of services. The health and social services need coefficients and the coefficient for services for older people will be determined annually for each wellbeing services county. They will describe the service needs of residents in the county in relation to other counties.

76. Transferring the responsibility for funding from municipalities to the central government will mean that the central government revenue will need to be increased and, at the same time, the revenue of municipalities will need to be reduced to correspond to the responsibility for funding transferred from them. To ensure the total tax ratio will not grow, all municipalities will be obliged to reduce local income tax. Municipal income tax percentages will be lowered by 12.39 percentage points for all municipalities when the relevant acts enter into force. Moreover, the municipalities‘ share of corporation tax revenue will be reduced, while the central government's share will be raised correspondingly. The changes in taxation will be as neutral as possible from the standpoint of taxpayers. The changes to the tax structure will not result in tax increases when the relevant acts enter into force.

77. The Ministry of Social Affairs and Health, the Ministry of the Interior and the Ministry of Finance will hold annual negotiations with each wellbeing services county. Each county will draw up an annual investment plan, and the Ministry of

45. Governmental decree on the organization and centralization of specialized care 582/2017, Valtioneuvoston asetus erikoissairaanhoidon … 582/2017 – Ajantasainen lainsäädäntö – FINLEX ®, 10 Sep. 2022.

Social Affairs and Health and the Ministry of the Interior will decide whether to approve it. An approved investment plan will be a requirement for new investments and asset transfers in the county.

78. The joint municipal authorities for hospital districts and for special care districts and their assets and liabilities will be transferred to the new wellbeing services counties. The wellbeing services counties will acquire the movable assets and contracts of the municipalities and joint municipal authorities relating to healthcare, social welfare and rescue services as well as the holiday pay liabilities of the transferable personnel without compensation.

79. The counties will lease municipality-owned facilities for healthcare, social welfare and rescue services for a transition period of three years with one year's option. Debts transferred from hospital districts and special care districts to the wellbeing services counties will be granted a government guarantee to safeguard the status of creditors and keep the loans in the zero-risk category. The transfers will be carried out based on reports drawn up by the municipalities and joint municipal authorities. Municipalities will be entitled to receive compensation for costs incurred in making asset arrangements when the direct costs exceed the entitlement threshold set by law. If the right of municipalities to decide on their own finances is compromised, they will be entitled to receive compensation even when the entitlement threshold is not exceeded.

Figure 2 The 21 Wellbeing Services Counties in Finland and Their Co-operation Areas[46]

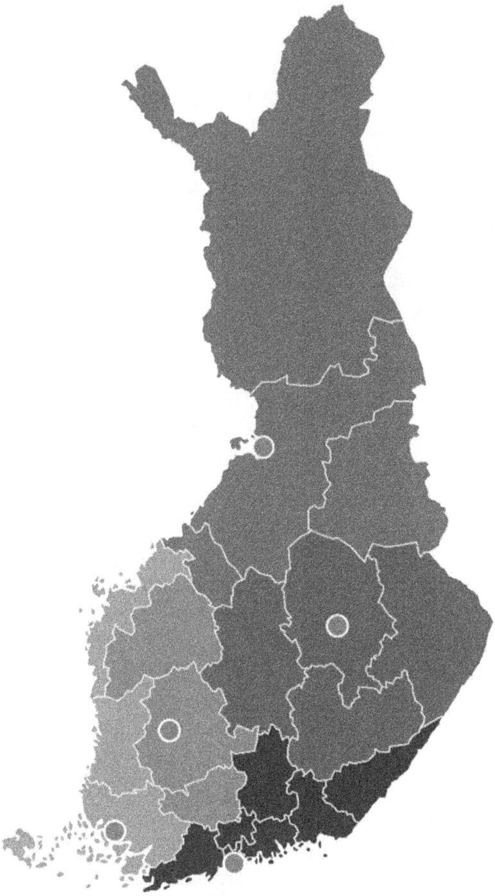

§3. SOURCES OF MEDICAL LAW IN FINLAND

80. Positioning of medical law within the judicial system has caused some difficulties among Finnish legal scholars as it has done also in many other countries.[47]

46. Sote-uudistus: Yhteistyöalueet, Yhteistyöalueet I Soteuudistus, 10 Sep. 2022.
47. Lahti, Raimo: Lääkintäoikeus–kehittyvä uusi tieteenala. Lakimies 1997:6,753-759.

Initially, there was a lot of academic activity related to medical law within researches of criminal law especially relating to the consent doctrine.[48] However, issues relating to medical law have also been studied in the field of administrative law where also the terms 'health law' or 'social law' are often used.[49] Patient competence issues and the rights of elderly people have been of interest to researchers of family law.[50] Medical injuries and their compensation have been of interest to some researchers of civil law.[51] Recently, also researchers of constitutional law have shown interest in medical law especially when considering health as a social right. Medical law teaching in some academic curriculums has been integrated into a new topic called 'welfare law', which includes legislation on different types of social benefits.[52] Medical law courses are available not only in law schools, but also in faculties educating students in social sciences. To some extent, courses may be available also in medical faculties in Finland especially as a part of specialist education or management courses.

81. Finland has pioneered legislation in support of patient's rights. In early 1980s, there were legislative initiatives for both no-fault compensation of medical damages and for strengthening patients' rights in healthcare.[53] The constitutional reforms in 1995 and 2000 further emphasized the basic rights of the people. Thus, the main sources of medical law are now in the national legislation and constitution. The chapter on basic rights in Finnish constitution was prepared to harmonize the basic rights in the Finnish constitution with the European Convention on Human Rights (ECHR) that Finland joined in 1989 after the collapse of Soviet Union. Looking retrospectively the past 50 years, it is evident that the development of medical law in Finland took place rather autonomously prior to the integration into the European legislative system.

82. In 1990s, there was, however, a strong emphasis on the international human rights conventions. Especially the Oviedo convention on Biomedicine in 1997 played an important role. It formed the basis for the Act on Medical Research of 1999 (488/1999) and also influenced deeply the Act on Infertility Treatments (1237/2006) of 2006. However, thereafter the importance of the international conventions for the national legislation has diminished and more emphasis has been on the impact of EU legislation. Especially the regulations on clinical trials, medical devices and on data protection have had a strong influence on praxis of medical law in Finland.

---

48. Anttila I: Loukatun suostumus oikeudenvastaisuuden poistavana perusteena: rikosoikeudellinen tutkimus. Suomalainen Lakimiesyhdistys 1946.
49. Lehtonen L, Lohiniva-Kerkelä M, Pahlman I: Terveysoikeus, Helsinki 2015.
50. Mäki-Petäjä-Leinonen A, Karvonen-Kälkänen A: Vanhusoikeuden perusteet, Alma Talent 2017; Hakalehto S: Lapsioikeuden perusteet. Alma Talent 2019.
51. Palonen R, Mustajoki P, Nio A: Potilas- ja lääkevahingot, Talentum 2005.
52. University of Eastern Finland: Studying welfare law, Studying Welfare Law – Hyvinvointioikeuden instituutti (uef.fi) Studies | Faculty of Law |, University of Lapland (ulapland.fi), 10 Sep. 2022.
53. Sosiaali- ja terveyshallinnon oikeusturvakomitean mietintö 1979:59; Sosiaali- ja terveyshallinnon oikeusturvakomitean mietintö 1981:64; Sosiaali- ja terveyshallinnon oikeusturvakomitean mietintö 1982:29.

83. There is little jurisprudence in Finland concerning classical issues of medical law. This is due to the fact that general courts are handling criminal cases and cases related to injuries, but not the decisions made by public authorities. However, healthcare is mostly part of the public administration in Finland and it is not common to sue a municipality or a healthcare district if you are not getting good care. Administrative court cases, on the other hand, in the field of medical law concentrate on the involuntary treatment of mental health patients.

84. The Finnish no-fault compensation system of medical injuries means that there is little need to go to court of law in the cases of medical negligence or injury. In Finland also the Parliamentary Ombudsman is supervising the basic rights of the people in public administration and his decisions are often compared to court cases when evaluating the actions of the authorities. The decisions of European Court of Human Rights (ECHR) are carefully followed in Finland. In some of its decisions, ECHR has found that the Finnish legislation on compulsory treatment of mental health patients is not giving adequate protection and demanded that the patients must have had right to second medical opinion and access to courts also in regard of the forms of medical treatment that are used in their care.[54] The decisions of ECHR have a big impact to the Finnish interpretation of human rights requirements in healthcare.

85. Constitutionality of parliamentary acts is checked in Finland as a part of the legislative process. The constitutional committee of the parliament reviews governments propositions for legislation and points out issues that do not fall within the limits set by the constitution. This was recently seen when the legislation for the control of the corona pandemic was evaluated in the Finnish parliament in 2020 and 2021. The statements of the constitutional committee on issues concerning e.g., consent, privacy and right to adequate health services form an important source for the interpretation of regulations of the healthcare in Finland.

54. ECHR Case of *X v. Finland* (Application no. 34806/04) Judgment Strasbourg 3 Jul. 2012 Final 19/11/2012, https://hudoc.echr.coe.int/eng#{%22itemid%22:[%22001-111938%22]}, 10 Sep. 2022.

Part I. The Medical Profession

Chapter 1. Access to the Medical Profession

§1. Training of Physicians

86. Finland had its first university, when Queen Christina founded The Royal Academy of Åbo in 1640, which was moved to Helsinki in 1828 by Czar Alexander I and is nowadays the University of Helsinki. The Academy had a medical faculty from the beginning and started medical education in Finland. However, most medical students continued their studies in other universities (e.g., in Uppsala in Sweden) and the number of medical doctors that graduated from the Academy was very limited.[55]

87. The University of Helsinki (or the Imperial Alexander University in Finland, from 1828 to 1919) had from 1833 onwards also a hospital (Clinical Institute) associated with it, which improved considerably medical teaching. University of Turku started medical education in 1943 and University of Oulu in 1958. The medical faculties in Tampere and Kuopio were established in 1972.

88. Access to medical education requires graduation from high schools. In 2021, about half of the students got access on the basis of their grades in the maturity examination and half of the students on the basis of the entrance exam. In the past, some universities also accepted a quota of registered nurses for medical studies. However, this system did not gain larger popularity and was later abolished.

89. Medical studies in the university take six years. If a medical doctor wants to specialise, he/she has to do a months months practice period in health centre as a part of the specialization. The postgraduation studies for a medical speciality take five or six years depending on the speciality. Furthermore, some 23% of the medical doctors in Finland also have a higher academic degree (Phd or Doctor of Medical Science).[56] The postgraduate academic studies usually take about four years before the dissertation.

55. Hyppölä H, Mattila K: Lääkärikoulutuksen historiaa ja nykytilanne Suomessa, Duodecim 2004;120:971–974, Lääkärikoulutuksen historiaa ja nykytilanne Suomessa (duodecimlehti.fi), 12 Sep. 2022.
56. Lääkäriliitto: Lääkärien määrä jatkaa edelleen kasvuaan, Lääkäriliitto – Lääkärien määrä jatkaa edelleen kasvuaan (laakariliitto.fi), 12 Sep. 2022.

§2. MANPOWER PLANNING

90. The Finnish constitution (section 16) guarantees the right to free basic education and promises that everybody has the access also to higher education without obstacles made by poverty. Furthermore, the same section also guarantees the freedom of science and higher education. This means that the universities can themselves decide the requirements for medical studies and the number of students they will take. However, the Ministry of Education and Culture funds the universities and can thus hugely influence the number of students in different faculties.

91. The number of medical doctors in Finland is lower than in other Nordic countries. The number of working age medical doctors in Finland in 2000 was about 16,000 and in 2020 about 22,000. Since the 2000s, the shortage of doctors has eased, and the ratio of physicians to population in Finland (4.6 per 1,000 population in 2018) is already above the EU average (3.8 per 1,000 population).[57]

92. Finland has five medical faculties (Helsinki, Turku, Tampere, Kuopio and Oulu) that annually take about 750 medical students, of which 99% finish their training. Furthermore, quite a few Finnish students go abroad for medical studies. This means that about 900 Finns graduate every year from medical schools. However, since about 600 medical doctors retire annually, the number of medical doctors in Finland is not increasing at a rate that would be needed to satisfy the demand for healthcare services. This is seen in long waiting times for patients.

93. Nurses greatly outnumber physicians in most OECD countries, and they play a critical role in providing healthcare not only in traditional settings such as hospitals and long-term care institutions but increasingly in primary care settings. The ratio of nurses to population in Finland (14.3 per 1,000 population in 2019) is the highest among EU countries.[58] The total number of social welfare and healthcare professionals has increased in Finland considerably during the past decade. In 2018, totally 457,000 people of working age had been granted the right to engage in social welfare and healthcare activities in comparison to 335,700 in 2010.[59] The role of nurses in primary care in Finland has gradually expanded and now includes limited prescribing and care coordination.

94. However, there are growing concerns in Finland about shortages of nurses, given that the demand for nurses is expected to rise in a context of population

57. The World Bank, Physicians per 1000 people – Finland, Physicians (per 1,000 people) – Finland | Data (worldbank.org) 12 Sep. 2022.
58. OECD: Availability of nurses, Availability of nurses | Health at a Glance: Europe 2020: State of Health in the EU Cycle | OECD iLibrary (oecd-ilibrary.org), 12 Sep. 2022.
59. The National Institute for Health and Welfare: Social and Healthcare Services in Finland 2018, Social and Healthcare Services in Finland 2018 (julkari.fi), 12 Sep. 2022.

ageing and the retirement of the current nurses.[60] In the 2000s, the number of personnel in the private sector and organizations has also increased faster than the number of personnel in the public sector.

§3. Licensing of Physicians

95. Since the seventeenth century, exercising of the professions of physician and pharmacist has been regulated in Finland (as a part of Sweden). The medical guild of Stockholm founded Collegium Medicorum in 1663 due to the faults caused by the practice of quackery. The guild was signed to supervise physicians, pharmacists and midwifes in the Stockholm area as well as to organize the medical assistance in the case of epidemic breaks. The privileges of Collegium were extended to cover the whole Swedish kingdom in 1668. In the eighteenth century, the Collegium was changed to a bureau in charge of the whole central administration. Similar bureau, Collegium Medicum, was founded by an imperial announcement in 1811 after Finland was incorporated into the Russian empire after the war of 1808–1809. In 1827, the bureau was changed to the National Board of Medical Practice and in 1878 to the National Board of Health. This office continued its practice until 1991. After that the National Authority for Medicolegal Affairs (in Finnish *Terveydenhuollon oikeusturvakeskus or TEO*) was in charge of the licenses and supervision of healthcare professionals from 1991 to 2008. Since 2008 it has been the task of National Supervisory Authority for Welfare and Health (in Finnish *Sosiaali- ja terveydenhuollon lupa ja valvontavirasto or Valvira*). This means that the Finnish healthcare professionals must have a license issued either by the National Board of Health, the Healthcare Supervision Centre or the National Supervisor Authority for Welfare and Health depending on the time of the graduation of the professional.

96. Physicians can apply their license after finishing their 6-year training in one of the five medical faculties in Finland. Specialty Training in Medicine and Dentistry in Finland is coordinated by the Ministry of Social Affairs and Health and organized by selected universities and hospitals in co-operation. There are altogether fifty different Specialty Training Programmes in Medicine and five in Dentistry. Prerequisites for training are a license to practice medicine or dentistry in Finland and a good command of the Finnish language.

97. The licensing of a profession is not totally in accordance with section 18 of the Finnish Constitution, which grants right to work in an occupation one prefers.[61] However, it is justified that the right to work in healthcare is regulated in order to protect the safety of the patients. Healthcare profession is subject to licensing also in other European countries and the common requirements within the EU are

60. Ensio A, Lammintakanen J, Härkönen M, Kinnunen J: Strengthening health systems through nursing: Evidence from 14 European countries – Finland, Finland – Strengthening health systems through nursing: Evidence from 14 European countries – NCBI Bookshelf (nih.gov) 12 Sep. 2022.
61. In the committee report 1992:3, which was part of the preparatory material of the basic rights reform of the Constitution in 1995, the issue was contemplated.

defined in Directive 2005/36/EC of the European Parliament and of the Council on the Recognition of the Professional Qualifications.

98. The Healthcare Professionals Act (559/1994) stipulates the right to practice profession in healthcare in Finland. Section 1 of the Act states that the objective of the Act is to promote the safety of patients and the quality of healthcare services. The Healthcare Professionals Act strives to ensure, that the people working within healthcare have the education and competence their profession requires. Section 2 defines the concept of healthcare professional in three different ways: as a person who, on the basis of the Healthcare Professionals Act, has been given the right to practice a profession (licensed professional) or as a person who, on the basis of the Act, is entitled to use the occupational title of a healthcare professional as laid down by Government decree (professional with a protected occupational title). In addition, National Supervisory Authority for Welfare and Health can, instead of licensing, give an authorization to practice the profession for foreigners, who are citizens of a country outside the EU or EEA (European Economic Area) and have been educated for the profession in a country outside the EU or EEA. These are called authorized healthcare professionals.

99. The right to operate as a licensed or authorized healthcare professional means that no one else than these professionals are entitled to perform tasks and duties included in the profession nor use the titles belonging to them. However, healthcare professionals with protected occupational titles can perform tasks and duties of other healthcare professionals, when his basic and updated training, experience and professional skills in the situation are appropriate, and if it is justifiable due to the work arrangements and production of healthcare services.[62]

100. The licensed healthcare professionals must wait for a licensing decision of supervisory authority (National Supervisory Authority for Welfare and Health) before they can practice the healthcare profession. Licensing is required in tasks, where healthcare professional operates so independently that the safety of patients requires specific professional skills; where the risks of treatment injury are higher than average; the contact with the patient is direct and includes actions that impact the patient both physically and mentally. Licensed healthcare professionals include the following professions: physician, dentist, qualified chemist, psychologist, speech therapist, dietician, pharmacist, nurse, midwife, public health nurse, physiotherapist, laboratory assistant, radiographer, dental hygienist, occupational therapist, optician and dental technician. In order for the professionals with protected occupational titles to use those titles, they must undergo a professional training or such. However, no separate license issued by supervisory authority is required.

101. Professionals, who on the basis of their education have a right to use protected occupational titles, are assistant nurse, rehabilitation tool technician, dental nurse, chiropodist, foot therapist, educated massage therapist, educated chiropractor, educated osteopath and naprapath, fitness nurse, childminder, practical nurse,

62. Lehtonen L, Lohiniva-Kerkelä M, Pahlman I: Terveysoikeus, Helsinki 2014.

porter-ambulance driver, mental health nurse, psychotherapist, hospital physicist, hospital geneticist, hospital chemist, hospital microbiologist and hospital cell-biologist. The terms *practical nurse* and *mental health nurse* include two different titles in Finnish. This is due to the fact that the education of practical and mental health nurses have changed during the years and so have the titles. In Finnish, the title *practical nurse* includes two titles: *perushoitaja* (previous degree) and *lähihoitaja* (the degree today). The tasks of the two different titles do not vary significantly. Both titles are protected occupational titles. The title of *mental health nurse* includes the two following titles: *mielisairaanhoitaja* (the previous degree) and *mielenterveyshoitaja* (the degree today). Both *mielisairaanhoitaja* and *mielenterveyshoitaja* are protected occupational titles.

102. The healthcare professionals with protected occupational titles are entitled to use their title on the basis of their education. Such are for example practical nurses, who have received their title after completing a so-called regulated training. Even though all professionals with protected occupational titles haven't sent their information to register maintained by National Supervisory Authority for Welfare and Health, they are still healthcare professionals as stipulated in the Healthcare Professionals Act.

103. Section 15 of the Healthcare Professionals Act forces the healthcare professional to constantly supplement their education. Section 18 of the Act obligates even more specifically that all healthcare professionals must maintain and advance the skills required in their position and familiarize themselves to the regulation considering their profession. Section 19 obligates all of them to follow the orders given by either National Supervisory Authority for Welfare and Health or Regional State Administrative Agency.

104. The language skill requirements demanded from healthcare professionals depend on the profession they practice. Also, to what language the skills are required depend on the place where at and on the profession professional practices. For example, in a health centre of a monolingual community, the language skill requirement differs whether the community is Swedish or Finnish speaking. Defective language skills may lead into supervisory actions.

105. Even though physician's, dentist's, qualified chemist's, nurse's and midwife's degree, which has been received in an either EU or EEA country, is automatically recognized without language skill requirements, section 18a of Healthcare Professionals Act stipulates that healthcare professionals must have sufficient language skills to practice their profession. Article 53 of the Recognition of Professional Qualifications Directive stipulates that professionals receiving advantage from automatic recognition must have such language skills that are required to practice the profession in the country receiving them. The article doesn't restrict the professionals' freedom to decide where to settle within the EU, but sets requirements to practice the profession in member countries.

106. While the labour is free to move in the EU, the conditions of competence and national licensing may become an obstacle for the common market to operate properly. That is why the European parliament and council have issued Directive 2005/36/EC on Recognition of the Professional Qualifications. In addition, the Nordic countries have made a separate agreement about a common labour market of certain healthcare personnel groups. The Directive has been implemented in Finland in the Recognition of the Professional Qualifications Act (1200/2007).

107. National Supervisory Authority for Welfare and Health is the national authority in Finland in charge of recognition of professional qualifications. From application, the authority automatically issues a license for those physicians, dentists, qualified chemists, nurses and midwifes, who have received their degree in another EU- or EEA-country than Finland. In addition, the authority automatically issues a license for those citizens of EU- or EEA-country, whose degree received outside EEA-area has already been recognized in some EU- or EEA-country.

108. The degrees to be recognized must fill the minimum standards presented in the Directive. For the part of other titles, the National Supervisory Authority for Welfare and Health grants a right to use a title from application for such a citizen of EU- or EEA-country who has been granted a diploma or similarly defined document about a degree that is required in that country for title.

109. If it is later discovered that the competence of the authorized foreigner is not sufficient and he has deficiencies in his education, the National Supervisory Authority for Welfare and Health may take actions to look into the competence of the authorized foreigner and possibly order him to take additional studies and tests to fill the gaps in his knowledge.[63]

110. Sections 6 and 7 in Healthcare Professionals Act stipulate that the recognition of the titles of physician, dentist, qualified chemist, nurse and midwife happens automatically, if the applicant has the diploma mentioned in the Directive's attachments. For the part of other healthcare professionals mentioned in the Act, the recognition system stipulated in section 8 of the Act is to be followed. Professionals included in the common recognition system must have a diploma or similar document that is required to grant the title in the country in question. The requirements of the diploma or similar document are more precisely stated in the Directive. The recognition system has five levels of competence, whose main criteria are the level,

63. *See National Supervisory Authority for Welfare and Health, number 1285/05.01.03.00/2009:* Several employers informed the National Supervisory Authority for Welfare and Health about their doubts of the competence of an authorized physician, who had received his degree abroad. The degree was received in an EU-country, so the Professional Qualifications Recognition Directive was applied to his authorization. National Supervisory Authority for Welfare and Health required that the physician in question took part in tests to evaluate his competence. The Medical Faculty, where the competence test of the physician in question was done, stated that on the basis of the test, the physician in question had severe deficiencies in his knowledge and competence, and thus he practicing profession in healthcare might endanger the safety of the patients. The physician was ordered to take additional training.

nature and length of the education. National Supervisory Authority for Welfare and Health may order the applicant into qualification test or put him on an adaption period. These measures do not violate the common recognition system. Section 5 paragraph 2 of the Recognition of the Professional Qualifications Act stipulates that the National Supervisory Authority for Welfare and Health may ask for, if needed, a statement about the congruence with the Finnish degree and possible missing topics in the original degree compared to the Finnish degree, from a university, school of applied sciences or another academy. The statement may also include opinions about the length of the adaption period, the contents of the tasks included in the adaption period and of the qualification test.

111. A degree received outside the EU/EEA-countries is recognized in Finland, if the conditions set in Healthcare Professionals Act are filled. This regulation considers all titles (including physicians and nurses). Section 11 of Healthcare Professionals Act stipulates that a degree received outside EU or EEA is recognized in Finland, if the National Supervisory Authority for Welfare and Health has approved the education leading to the degree. Before the Authority has approved the education leading to the degree, it cannot demand the applicant to perform any further studies or attend any tests. Similar procedure is applied to a person, who is not of an EU or EEA nationality. Sufficient skills in Finnish or Swedish are also demanded from a person, who has received his degree outside the EU or EEA. One must note that the Authority can't set any language demands for physicians, dentists, nurses and so on who are within the automatic recognition system stipulated in the Professional Qualifications Recognition Directive. The control in this matter is in the hands of the employer.

112. In addition to the above mentioned, a professional who has legally settled into an EU- or EEA-country, has a legal right to practice his profession independently and provide the services included in his profession, that are stipulated in section 9 of the Healthcare Professionals Act, in Finland temporarily or occasionally. However, he has to make a prior notice in writing for National Supervisory Authority for Welfare and Health.

Chapter 2. The Practice of Medicine

§1. Act of Healthcare Professionals

113. There is no exclusive definition of medical activities in Finland. The practices performed by various professions change with time. Many activities that were carried out by medical doctors in the past are carried now out by other healthcare professionals. Furthermore, many activities that were solely carried out by healthcare professionals, can now be carried out by the patients themselves. If the patient is able to do the procedure himself (e.g., measuring blood pressure, injecting insulin etc.), it is possible also for a lay person to do the same for the patient with the consent of the patient. Lay persons, however, are not allowed to market their services and claim to be professionals or adequately educated for these tasks.

114. A licensed healthcare professional or professional with protected occupational title can temporarily perform tasks of another healthcare professional, if it is needed due to work arrangements or for better healthcare service production, and if the tasks are similar to his education, experience and competence. In addition, a student studying to become a healthcare professional may temporarily work in his/her area of education. The right of students to work in tasks of healthcare professionals is described in section 3 of the Decree on Healthcare Professionals (564/1994).

115. The National Supervisory Authority for Welfare and Health is keeping a central register of healthcare professionals. The register contains the following information on healthcare professionals:

- name, personal identity code, registration number, home address, right to practice a profession and restrictions on it or its withdrawal, authorization to practice a profession or its cancellation, right to use an occupational title of a healthcare professional and its prohibition, and information on the training on which the right or authorization to practice a profession or to use a protected title is based;
- any decision of the National Supervisory Authority for Welfare and Health and a Regional State Administrative Agency indicating that erroneousness, neglect or reprehensibility has been perceived in the professional activity of a professional, as well as information on any reprimands, fines or sentences of imprisonment related to the practice of the profession, dismissal or suspending from office;
- identification code and information on the right to practice as medical or dental specialist and on the training that it is based on, information on the specific training in general medical practice or comparable training completed by a physician, information on the specific qualifications of a healthcare professional and on the training that it is based on, and information on the healthcare unit where a nurse has a limited right to prescribe medicines;
- name, personal identity code, registration number, date of start of studies and information on the completed studies of medical, dental or pharmacy students who have completed the studies laid down in this Act and the Government decree issued in virtue of it;

- information on the name, personal identity code and address of a student for healthcare profession that has been subject of disciplinary actions by the National Supervisory Authority for Welfare and Health or by Regional State Administrative Agency; and
- information on the acceptance of a physician for the follow-up of the personnel in radiation work.

116. The information referred to will be removed from the register in ten years after the National Supervisory Authority for Welfare and Health has received information about the death of a registered person or in two years after the temporary or occasional provision of healthcare services has ended. Furthermore, the information on disciplinary actions will be removed after ten years have passed from the issuing of the decision or equivalent.

117. The National Supervisory Authority for Welfare and Health may, notwithstanding the confidentiality provisions, give authorities and healthcare units information about the criminal sanctions of the healthcare professionals that are stored in the central registry. Concerning the assessment of a job seeker, the National Supervisory Authority for Welfare and Health may give from the central register information, in the form of copies or in electronic form, on names and addresses of persons entered into the register, as well as information on their right and authorization to practice a profession and on their training.

118. Section 24b of the Healthcare Professionals Act stipulates that the National Supervisory Authority for Welfare and Health can give information to the public from the register. The National Supervisory Authority for Welfare and Health may submit via a public information network, information on a healthcare professional's name, registration number, year of birth and the professional qualifications of a professional as well as about restrictions on the person's right to practice a profession (public information service). Furthermore, public information service may include information on the name, registration number, year of birth and date of start of studies of medical, dental or pharmacy students entitled to practice as a licensed healthcare professional. Information from public information service may only be sought in the form of individual searches by using the name or registration number of the registered person. The National Supervisory Authority for Welfare and Health will remove the information on a healthcare professional from public information service immediately after it has received information about the professional's death or after the right of the healthcare professional to practice a profession has been withdrawn, the authorization to practice a profession has been cancelled or the use of an occupational title has been prohibited.

119. Thus, anyone can check the competence of a healthcare professional from a public information service form of the Terhikki-register called Julki-Terhikki.[64] The information contained in Julki-Terhikki is updated once a day.

120. The most important regulations concerning the practice of medicine in Finland are in the Act on Healthcare Professionals (559/1994). Even though the act concerns all professionals working in healthcare, it has many specific rules for physicians.

121. The act aims to promote patient safety and quality of services by requiring adequate professional qualifications for healthcare personnel. It also has regulations concerning the supervision of healthcare personnel. The tasks performed by healthcare professionals must, as a rule, be equivalent to the commonly demanded professional standard in healthcare for the competence and education demands of the task. The tasks of the healthcare professionals change whilst healthcare develops and the contents of the education changes.

122. The third chapter of the Act on Healthcare Professionals states the general obligations of the professionals. The aim of their work should always be the maintenance and promotion of health, prevention of disease as well as curing illnesses and relieving the suffering of the diseased. The healthcare professionals should according to section 15 of the Act always apply generally accepted and empirically based methods in accordance with their education. They should also maintain and supplement their professional training. This obligation is also stipulated in section 18 of the Act. Furthermore, the employer of the healthcare professional should follow the professional development and make the participation to supplementary training possible. The employers should also verify that healthcare professionals have adequate language skills for their tasks.

123. The healthcare professionals should balance the benefits and potential harms of their activities for the patients. The professionals have a specific obligation to take into consideration the regulations for the Act on the Status and Rights of the Patients (the Patient's Rights Act). If there is a need of urgent care, healthcare professionals must give treatment to the patient regardless of patient's race, religion, political opinion, social status or other thing considering patient's person. section 16 of the Act on Healthcare Professionals states that the preparation and retention of patient documents is stipulated in section 12 of the Patient's Rights Act and in the Decree about Patient Documents given by the Ministry of Social Affairs and Health.[65]

---

64. National Supervisory Authority for Welfare and Health: Registers of social welfare and healthcare professionals, https://julkiterhikki.Valvira.fi/Default.aspx?lang=fi JulkiTerhikki (valvira.fi), 16 Sep. 2022.
65. Sosiaali- ja terveysministeriön asetus potilasasiakirjoista, Sosiaali- ja terveysministeriön asetus … 94/2022 – Säädökset alkuperäisinä – FINLEX ®, 16 Sep. 2022.

124. The healthcare professionals have to maintain health records as stipulated in the Patient's Rights Act. They are also obliged to inform authorities on births and deaths. Section 1 of the Act on Investigation for the Reason of Death (1065/2009) states that healthcare units and physicians should send notification on deaths to population data system and to National Institute for Health and Welfare (THL).

125. All healthcare professionals are bound by confidentiality requirements. According to section 15 of the Act on Healthcare Professionals, they are not allowed to disclose to outsiders any secrets of a private person or family that they have learned in their professional activities. This confidentiality requirement stays in force even if the healthcare professional is not working anymore in healthcare. It is crucial to note, that this confidentiality requirement doesn't include just information in patient documents but everything the patient wishes to keep as secret.

126. If the physician wants to work as an independent practitioner, he/she has to notify the Regional State Administrative Agency (AVI) on the premises before the activities start as stated in Act on Private Healthcare (152/1990). Furthermore, he/she has to take the obligatory patient insurance for potential damages as stated in the Act on Patient Insurance (948/2019).

127. The specific rights and obligations of the physician and dentist are listed in Chapter 4 of the Act on Healthcare Professionals. According to section 22 of the Act, a licensed physician has the right to decide the appropriate examinations, make diagnosis and to decide the medical therapy for the patient. A dentist has the same rights for dental patients. It should, however, be noted that even though the physician has the privilege to decide on medical therapies, they cannot be given without the consent of the patient.

128. The licensed physician has the right to make prescriptions for pharmaceuticals for medical use and a dentist for dental use. The physician and dentist should use a specific identification number (SV-tunnus), when making the prescriptions. Section 23 of the Act on Healthcare Professionals stipulates that nurse, who have sufficient practical experience and have completed the additional training prescribed by Government degree, have a limited right to prescribe from a pharmacy the medicines used in the treatment for the patients they are treating at the health centre. The other requirements for the nurse prescription include that it considers preventive care or continued medication where a physician has previously made the diagnosis or the medication is based on the need for treatment as assessed by the nurse. In addition, opticians and oral hygienists practicing the profession independently have the right to prescribe medicines obtained from a pharmacy that are needed in connection with the care provided by them.

129. Licensed physicians and dentists can give medical statements and certificates to courts and authorities. Section 23 of the Act on Healthcare Professionals stipulates the healthcare professional's duties to give medicolegal certificates and statements. Usually, medicolegal statements are asked for governmental benefit applications. Benefits are paid e.g., if the possibility to work has declined due to illness, defect or disability. The Act on Healthcare Professionals does not set any obligations as such to healthcare professionals to write medicolegal certificates and statements for their patients. This obligation is more of a result of healthcare professionals' common obligations to promote patient's interest and to work according to good medical practice. Official duties may also result in the obligation to write a medicolegal certificate or statement. In addition, there are other specific legislations which include provisions about the certificate-writing duties of other physicians than physicians holding and office (e.g., the Inquest Act 1973/459). Physicians (and other authorized professionals) do not have to swear an oath and be personally present for testifying in a court of law, if they have verified the certificate according to the section 23 of the Act with a specific statement 'which I affirm through my honor and conscience'.

130. The medicolegal certificate or statement must be based on such information that the writer of the statement or certificate is certain. This means that the certificate cannot be based only on the story told by the patient but for example on the physician's own observations made of the patient (e.g., clinical study, findings of laboratory tests or x-ray pictures), previous notes made by the physician or information received from other healthcare units. The stories of relatives and outsiders can be used as background information, but they cannot be the basis of the certificate or statement. The necessary personal information of the patient must be clearly stated in the certificate or statement so that the person may easily be specified.

131. The medicolegal certificate or statement must include all necessary information which is the basis of the made conclusions, not just the ones that are profitable for the patient. In broad certificates (e.g., Medicolegal certificate B used in evaluation of disability to work) the anamnesis of the patient and the objective observations must be so perfectly written that another physician may conclude whether he can agree with them or not.

§2. Private Healthcare Act

132. Private healthcare has become more important during the past two decades in Finland. The social and healthcare reform tries to turn this development and emphasizes the main role of public healthcare in the Finnish system. Non-Governmental Organizations have during the past two decades more or less lost their position as service healthcare providers, but different patient associations still do health promotion and patient education work. Private healthcare in Finland in 2020s is mainly run by three nationwide companies (Mehiläinen, Pihlajalinna and Terveystalo) that hire doctors to work as employees or as entrepreneurs in their premises. In 2016, some 30% of the Finnish doctors had their main occupancy in the private sector.[66] In some specialties, like ophthalmology and gynaecology, appointments in private healthcare form the majority of patient visits. There are also some private hospitals for orthopaedic surgery in Finland. However, for more serious conditions, public hospitals form the basis of care in all specialties and for emergency care.

133. According to Private Healthcare Act (152/1990), a provider of private healthcare services is a person or company, co-operative, association or another corporation or foundation, which maintains a unit providing healthcare services. Healthcare unit is a functional ensemble, which offers healthcare services. Section 2 of Private Healthcare Act stipulates that the following are considered as healthcare services: laboratory functions, radiological functions, examinations made to estimate health or to make a diagnosis of illness or to prescribe a treatment, physiotherapeutic functions and massage, occupational healthcare and dental and medical services. In addition, patient transportation services require a license for private healthcare.

134. The National Supervisory Authority for Welfare and Health and Regional State Administrative Agencies maintain together a national register of private healthcare services providers. The register has been created to process easily license and notification matters and to supervise and to compile statistics of operations. The information services include a separate register on private healthcare service providers and self-employed healthcare professionals and a separate register on private social services providers. The licensing authority saves the information on license application to the register, as well as information about changes in operations. Also, information about possible situations where the laws and provisions, orders and guidance based on legislation have been broken and their consequences will be stored in the registry. The National Supervisory Authority for Welfare and Health can publish and hand over the names or business names of healthcare service providers, information about their service branch and all addresses and contact addresses of their offices from the register through public information network.

135. The Regional State Administrative Agencies save the information contained in the notifications as stipulated in section 9a on Private Healthcare Act about self-employed healthcare professionals. In addition, information about the scale of the operations and their changes, possible breach of orders and prohibitions and their consequences to a self-employed healthcare professional are stored to the register. A self-employed healthcare professional will be removed from the register after five years have passed since he ended his practice.

136. Section 4 of Private Healthcare Act stipulates that in order to provide healthcare services as a private entrepreneur or by a non-profit corporation, one must have a license issued by National Supervisory Authority for Welfare and Health (Valvira). If the services are offered within a field of operation of just single

66. Lääkäriliitto: Lääkärit Suomessa, https://www.laakariliitto.fi/site/assets/files/5223/ll16_tilasto2016_net1_170114.pdf, 17 Sep. 2022.

Regional State Administrative Agency, the Agency in question can issue the license. But if the operations cover more than just one region, the license for healthcare services delivery must be issued by the National Supervisory Authority for Welfare and Health.

The license application must include:

- business name, logo, business identification number and contact information;
- the units offering healthcare services and their locations;
- the service sector and the contents and extent of the healthcare services provided;
- the name, personal identification number, education, profession and contact information of the director in charge of healthcare services;
- the name, education, profession and contact information of the patient ombudsman;
- the education and the number of staff;
- information about registration to Employer Register;
- information about the repository of patient documents, account on the main principles of keeping of a patient register and information about the person in charge of the register; and
- For necessary parts, information about the equipment and material used, and other requisite information about the quality, safety and regularity of the services provided.

137. In addition to abovementioned, the name and contact information of managing director or other person in charge of the business must be included. The change of director in charge of healthcare services requires the approval of licensing authority (a notification on amendment).

138. The license isn't required when healthcare services are provided as self-employed healthcare professional or when employer offers services of occupational health. Self-employed healthcare professional is defined as a healthcare professional, who independently practices his profession. Section 9a of Private Healthcare Act stipulates that to start practice as self-employed healthcare professional, one must send a written notice to Regional State Administrative Agency before starting the practice. The notice must be sent to that Regional State Administrative Agency on whose field of operation the services mainly will be provided.

139. The application to provide private healthcare services must be done in good time before starting the operations. Before the license has been issued, no services can be provided. Furthermore, section 8 of Private Healthcare Act stipulates that the provider of healthcare service must make a written notification to licensing authority about the starting of operations. The notification must include an auditor's report (or on special grounds, some other sufficient account) and a plan for the supervision of the services.

140. If the healthcare services provider essentially changes the services or stops providing them, the provider must make a written notification about the matter to the licensing authority. On special grounds, the licensing authority may obligate the provider to apply for new license if the change on the services is very extensive.

141. Section 3 of Private Healthcare Act demands that proper spaces and equipment must be used when providing private healthcare services. Operations must be medically approvable and take patent safety into account. In addition, service provider must have a properly educated staff. The education of the staff must be related to the services provided. Patient transportation provider must have proper ambulance with required equipment.

142. The service provider must let the board of healthcare audit the spaces and equipment or ambulance and its equipment before putting them in operation. More precisely, the auditing will be done by an office-bearer working for the board of health in the area, where the services will be provided. Usually, the auditing is performed by a responsible physician, dentist or other person, who knows the business in hand, either alone or with an office-bearer in charge of environment hygiene. The auditor's report must be signed by responsible physician or dentist of health centre (Ministry of Social Affairs and Health, Decree on Private Healthcare 744/1990).

143. The auditor will give the auditor's report to the service provider in order to make possible improvements to the spaces and equipment. The service provider must make a written notification to the licensing authority about starting the operations before starting them. Auditor's report (or on special grounds, other sufficient account) and the plan for the supervision of the services must be attached to the notification.

144. In addition, National Supervisory Authority for Welfare and Health or Regional State Administrative Agency can audit the operations and the units and office spaces of the service providers when it is done for justifiable reason. The audit can be made without prior notice. Section 17 of the Private Healthcare Act stipulates that the auditor must have access to all spaces of the office in question. All documents that the auditor asks for must be presented without any confidentiality clause restrictions if it is necessary for the audit.

145. The service provider must have a director in charge of healthcare services who has been approved by the licensing authority. The director in charge of healthcare services must be a healthcare professional as stipulated in section 2 of the Act on Healthcare Professionals, who has an education and practical experience required to successfully fulfil the tasks as the extent and services of the operations provided require.

146. After the operations have started, it is the task of the director in charge of healthcare services to make sure that the operations function according to the laws and obligations set for healthcare services. When providing healthcare services, the director in charge of healthcare services is responsible that:

- the operations fulfil the obligations set in legislation, and the orders and regulation based on legislation;
- the amount, education and competence of the staff is sufficient and the spaces and equipment function appropriately;
- the operations are medically justifiable, of high-quality and safe for patients;
- the patient documents are written and maintained properly;
- reprimands are handled appropriately; and
- the service provider makes notifications on amendments and annual reports to licensing authority.

147. The director in charge of healthcare services is also responsible for other administrative issues, for example making sure that annual report is made of the operations and then delivered to Regional State Administrative Agency. If the director in charge of healthcare services neglects his supervision duties or is in some other way incapable to take care of his tasks, Regional State Administrative Agency or National Supervisory Authority for Welfare and Health can cancel the approval of director in charge of healthcare services.

148. The director in charge of healthcare services must also make sure that the equipment fulfils the requirements set in legislation, that they are properly maintained, and used according to the manufacturer's directions. Section 18 of the Act on Equipment and Materials used in Healthcare (720/2021) and section 49 of the Act on Medical Devices (719/2021) require that the professional user of the medical equipment and devices must inform Finnish Medicines Agency (Fimea) of dangerous situations caused by features of materials or equipment, deviation on capacity or by insufficient marking or directions. Notification must also be done when the role of the equipment in the situation is unclear. The manufacturer or his representative must also be informed about the dangerous situation.

149. If the service provider uses pharmaceuticals to provide treatment, the director in charge of healthcare services must make sure that the office in question has an appropriate plan for their use, as well.[67] A code of conduct must be added to the plan on the supervision of the services. It must include procedural guidance about how medicinal treatment and the consumption of medicines are supervised, and what procedure is to be followed when exceptions are made from the medicinal treatment plan.

150. A hygiene plan of the healthcare provider must include used hygiene practices, which include hand hygiene, aseptic actions, maintenance and sterilizing of instruments, cleaning, laundry, isolation of patients and follow-up of infections. The people in charge of prevention of infections and their tasks must be clearly stated at the hygiene plan.

---

67. Sosiaali- ja terveysministeriö: Turvallinen lääkehoito – opas lääkehoitosuunnitelman laatimiseen, Sosiaali- ja terveysministeriön julkaisuja 2021:6, Turvallinen lääkehoito: Opas lääkehoitosuunnitelman laatimiseen–Valto (valtioneuvosto.fi), 17 Sep. 2022.

151. Cleaning that is involved with the services provided must be planned, and the plan attached to the plan on the supervision of services. In addition, especially for hospital wards and rehabilitation, the service plan for meals and nutrition must be attached.

152. A description of waste management procedures and toxic waste processing procedures must be attached to the plan. Special attention must be paid to the processing procedures of possibly infectious waste.

153. The director in charge of private healthcare services must give written instructions about the processing and handing over information in patient documents. The instructions must be attached to the plan on the supervision of services. Special attention must be paid to procedures that involve the registered person's right to check and correct information considering him and to the organization of informing of the registered person. The service provider, who handles personal information electronically, must have a named person in charge for data protection.

154. The Patient's Rights Act (785/1992) requires that every healthcare unit has a patient ombudsman. The ombudsman's name, education, contact information, how and when he can be met, and how the information about patient ombudsman must be kept available to the patients and it must be included in the plan on the supervision of services. In order to assure the independence and impartiality of patient ombudsman, the director in charge of healthcare services cannot be the patient ombudsman. The principles of patient ombudsman's actions and, for example, the information he possibly has gathered from the received feedback, are included into the plan.

155. Section 10 of the Patient's Rights Act stipulates that a patient not satisfied with the received treatment and care has a right to make a complaint. The plan must include a code of conduct on how to reply to complaints. The director in charge of healthcare services is responsible for the proper and careful handling of complaints.

156. The director in charge of the service is responsible to create a feedback system for complaints. This includes instructions to the staff on how the feedback should be processed. The procedures used in case of treatment injury and the guidance given to staff in those cases must be included into the plan on the supervision of services. The director in charge must take care of the guidance. He is also in charge of deciding who will be in charge of delivering the asked information to Finnish Patient Insurance Centre.

157. It is the duty of director in charge of healthcare services to update the plan on the supervision of the services. If it is discovered that there are defects or flaws in the organization and the implementation of healthcare services or the operations are in some other way against the law, the National Supervisory Authority for Welfare and Health or Regional State Administrative Agency may give an order to rectify the defects or to remove the flaws as stipulated in section 20 of Private Healthcare Act. After the authority has given the order, it must set a deadline for the healthcare services provider to do the required measures. If patient safety so requires, operations may be ordered to be suspended or the usage of a healthcare unit, completely or partially, or of an ambulance or its equipment or tools may be forbidden immediately. The authority may back up its order by adding a risk to a fine or by stating that the operations will be suspended or that the usage of the healthcare unit or an ambulance will be forbidden.

158. Section 21 of Private Healthcare Act stipulates that the licensing authority may also revoke the license it has issued to provide healthcare services, if the operations have grossly broken the Act or the guidance that supervisory authorities have given.

§3. Act on Occupational Healthcare

159. One of the peculiar features of the Finnish healthcare system is the prominent role of occupational healthcare. In practice, the employers are providing their workforce with health services that officially should be provided by the public health system. Occupational healthcare is thus forming an alternative system for health services for Finns with an employment. It, however, creates additional issues in medical law since the practicing physician (who is paid by the employer) must consider both the interests of the employer and employee in the practice of medicine.

160. Occupational healthcare is an important part of primary healthcare services in Finland. According to the Act on Occupational Healthcare (1383/2001), the purpose of occupational healthcare is to promote work safety, health and ability to work of employees. Section 1 of Act on Occupational Healthcare (1383/2001) stipulates that the main objective of the act is, in co-operation between employer, employee and occupational healthcare, to prevent work-related illnesses and injuries, to promote health and safety of work and work environment, as well as the health of employees.

161. The Act on Occupational Healthcare obligates employer to organize healthcare services to prevent work-related illnesses to his/her employees. For those purposes, employer uses the experts and healthcare professionals of occupational healthcare service providers. The obligation to organize occupational healthcare services includes all public and private employments regardless of the company type of the employer, of how the employment is organized and of how long the employment has lasted. Entrepreneur can organize his/her own occupational healthcare, but section 12 of the Act stipulates that it is optional.

162. Section 7 of the Act on Occupational Healthcare stipulates that employer can organize occupational healthcare services either by him/herself or with other employers. Employer can acquire services from such a health centre or from other unit or person who has been licensed to provide occupational healthcare services.

163. Chapter 13 of Health Insurance Act (1224/2004) stipulates that the costs of occupational healthcare will be compensated. The compensation will be paid for costs of occupational healthcare and for other costs caused by the obligation of employer to organize occupational healthcare, such as medical costs. The compensation is also paid for occupational healthcare services the employer has organized for himself/herself. In principle, 50% of the costs are compensated.

164. The employer must use sufficiently the healthcare professionals and experts they consider necessary in matters concerning the planning, producing, development and follow-up of occupational healthcare. The need for human resources depends on the health and safety of work and the working circumstances. It must also be noted when defining the need for staff whether the employer has included other healthcare services to occupational healthcare services or not.

165. Section 3 of the Act on Occupational Healthcare stipulates that occupational healthcare services provider is defined either as an organization or a person who takes care of the occupational healthcare services that the employer is either obligated to organize or he/she voluntarily organizes. The conditions to organize occupational healthcare services are stipulated in for example the Private Healthcare Act and in the Act on Healthcare Professionals.

166. The employer and the occupational healthcare services provider must make a written agreement on producing occupational healthcare services. The agreement must include provisions about the common organization of occupational healthcare services and the width and content of the services. If the employee or entrepreneur organizes also other healthcare services, an agreement must be made of them with the occupational healthcare services provider as stipulated in section 14 of the Act on Occupational Healthcare.

167. Employer or entrepreneur can organize other healthcare services in addition to occupational healthcare services. If he/she decides to do so, a written agreement must be made with the occupational healthcare services provided as stipulated in section 14 of the Act on Occupational Healthcare.

168. Even though the employer is in charge of organizing occupational healthcare services, employer must work in co-operation with employees and occupational healthcare services provided as stipulated in section 8 of Act on Occupational Healthcare (so-called principle of co-operation). Before the employer decides how the occupational healthcare services are to be organized or decides about another important fact affecting the occupational healthcare services, the matter must be handled in work safety committee as stipulated in Act on the Supervision of Occupational Safety and Appeal in Occupational Safety Matters, or on co-operation procedure replacing such a committee. In practice, the principle of co-operation means that employees and their representatives have the possibility to make suggestions to develop occupational healthcare services and receive expert help to determine how much the work strains them or of other matter affecting the health of employees.

169. Section 12 of Act on Occupational Healthcare stipulates that occupational healthcare services must include:

- investigation and assessment of the healthiness and safety of the work;
- investigation, assessment and monitoring of work-related health risks and problems, employees' health, working capacity and functional capacity;
- giving information, consulting and guidance;
- monitoring and supporting the ability of a disabled employee to cope at work;
- assessment of ability to work and of ability to function and giving statements;
- co-operation with representatives of other healthcare services, labour authorities, educational authorities, social insurance, social services and the occupational safety and health authority;
- participation in organizing the first aid referred to in section 46 of the Occupational Safety and Health Act;
- assistance in planning and organizing measures to maintain and promote working ability; and
- assessment and monitoring of the quality and impact of occupational healthcare activities.

170. Occupational healthcare services must be organized with good occupational healthcare practice. Good occupational healthcare practice is defined as common principles followed in organizing, producing and developing of occupational healthcare services with consideration of the knowledge and experience of occupational health. Good occupational healthcare practice also includes good professional practice, multi-scientific and multi-professional operations, required information about work conditions and the co-operation required in the Act on Occupational Healthcare.

171. The item 3 of paragraph 1 of section 13 of Act on Occupational Healthcare stipulates that compulsory health examinations can be made when an employee has normal ability to function but work is such that it has effects on health which must be cleared or when the work is ordinary, but the healthcare of employee is such that it must be found out whether he/she can stand the demands of work. This means that employee can be ordered to compulsory health examination either on work or employee-based reasons. Employee can be ordered to health examination either when she/he is starting the work or when she/he is already working.

172. The section 13 of Act on Occupational Healthcare stipulates that a certificate must be drafted of health examination, and it must include estimation about whether the healthcare of the employee suits for the tasks he/she is to take to. A common estimation is made by the physician by the using expressions proper, not proper or proper when made with necessary restrictions.

Chapter 3. Illegal Practice of Medicine

173. Illegal practice of medicine is not very common in Finland. It is relatively easy to check from the Finnish universities that a physician has finished his/her training and got his/her diploma, and this is also regularly done by the hospitals, when they recruit staff. The biggest irregularities are related to students who have a temporary license to practice and do not finish their training in time, as well as foreign staff that has unclear or forged diplomas. The National Supervisory Authority for Welfare and Health (Valvira) is checking the diplomas of immigrant workers, but it is often slow and cumbersome to get the confirmation from universities outside Europe.[68]

174. The illegal practice of medicine is criminalized in the Finnish Criminal Code. Section 3 in Chapter 44 of the Criminal Code states that the punishment for unlicensed practice of healthcare profession is either fine or imprisonment for maximally six months.[69] Since unlicensed, and thus illegal, practice is causing danger not only to individual patient, but to the general population, the crime is an indictable offence which is not dependent on the activity of the patient in question to press charges.

175. There is, however, a grey area between the practice of a healthcare profession and various wellbeing services. This is seen especially with different types of therapies for mental health. Even though giving psychotherapy is restricted to healthcare professionals, the word 'therapy' can be used for various alternative services that intend to make you feel better (e.g., aromatherapy).[70] This sometimes creates confusion (especially if healthcare professionals are involved with alternative therapies). In Finland, the problems in the quality and price of alternative 'therapies' are mainly turned to consumer protection authorities instead of the supervisory authority Valvira.[71] Consumer protections authorities, on the other hand, mainly supervise the marketing of the services, meaning that the marketing of the services that are provided by a lay person is not promising a potential cure for a medical condition. This type of marketing is allowed only for proper healthcare professionals.

176. In a criminal process concerning illegal practice of medicine, the courts rely much on the expert opinion of the National Supervisory Authority for Welfare and Health (Valvira), whether an activity belongs to the protected sphere or whether

68. National Supervisory Authority for Welfare and Health: Qualified outside the EU/EEA Member State, https://www.valvira.fi/web/en/healthcare/professional_practice_rights/qualified_outside_the_eu_eea_member_state, 17 Sep. 2022.
69. The Finnish Supreme Court, KKO:2010:14: A technician making lenses for eyeglasses had carried out visual examinations without license to work as a healthcare professional. He was sentenced to fines.
70. Yle: Kuka tahansa voi nimittää itsensä terapeutiksi, Kuka tahansa voi nimittää itsensä terapeutiksi | Yle Uutiset | yle.fi, 17 Sep. 2022.
71. Finnish Competition and Consumer Authority: Miracle products, https://www.kkv.fi/en/consumer-affairs/scams/miracle-products/, 17 Sep. 2022.

it is open for other staff than healthcare professionals. There have been some cases in Finland, where a person has pretended to be a doctor or nurse without appropriate training. In one case, a prison sentence over five years was sentenced for a 'fake doctor' with damages of over EUR 1 million.[72] In this case, the longest terms of imprisonment were based on fraud and forgery and not just for illegal healthcare practice stipulated in paragraph 3 of section 44 of the Finish Criminal Code. He was also found guilty for abuse, since the intrusion of physical integrity is not allowed for persons without a medical license. The illegal practice of medicine can thus fulfil the criteria of various crimes (fraud, forgery, abuse) in addition to the criteria set in the actual paragraph for illegal practice.

177. In the cases of fake nurses or doctors, the employers that have learnt that the person does not have qualifications to work as a healthcare professional have usually demanded compensation for the salaries i.e., the person in question has been obliged to pay back either the whole salary or the difference between a student's salary and qualified professional. Very rarely there has been any patient injuries that would have justified compensation for the patients.

72. Yle: Hovioikeus kovensi valelääkäri Esa Laihon tuomiota – 5 vuotta ehdotonta vankeutta ja Laiho heti vangittavaksi, Hovioikeus kovensi valelääkäri Esa Laihon tuomiota – 5 vuotta ehdotonta vankeutta ja Laiho heti vangittavaksi | Yle Uutiset | yle.fi, 17 Sep. 2022.

Chapter 4. Control of the Practice of Medicine

§1. Professional Liability

I. Civil Liability

178. Finland established a non-fault compensation system for medical injuries in 1980s. Therefore, civil liability cases in courts against healthcare professionals are quite rare in Finland. However, it is possible to go to court for damages as well.

179. The original Act on Patient Injuries from 1986 was replaced in 2019 with the Patient Insurance Act (948/2019). The Act applies to all healthcare that is provided in Finland and also to healthcare that is arranged abroad but which is under responsibility of the municipalities or regions and is necessary for the health of the patients. It is mandatory for all healthcare professionals to work under patient insurance policy (section 6 of the Act). The only exception is emergency care that a healthcare professional is obliged to give even though he/she would not have a valid insurance policy.

180. The minimum terms of the insurance are also defined in the Act. The insurance fees have to be uniform for all clients of the insurance giver and have to take into consideration the risk for patient injuries as well as the adequate cover needed for the insured.

181. Finnish Insurance companies have established a specific unit (Patient Insurance Centre),[73] to handle the insurance claims. There are about 9,000 claims made annually, of which some 25%-30% are compensated according to the Act.[74] If a healthcare professional has neglected to take the mandatory insurance, the damages will be covered by Patient Insurance Centre that is then demanding the neglected fees with sanctions from the professional or healthcare unit in question.

182. According to the Patient Insurance Act, the patient has a right to compensation, if he/she has experienced personal damage fulfilling the criteria in the section 23 of the Act. The amount of compensation is based on Tort Liability Act (412/1974). It should be noted, however, that Patient Insurance Act covers only those damages that are not compensated on the bases of some other legislation. This means that compensations from patient insurance is secondary to the general social welfare.

183. Eight compensation criteria are listed in the Patient Insurance Act. *A treatment injury* is the most common compensable injury. A compensable treatment injury is a bodily injury which was caused by an examination, treatment or other

73. Patient Insurance Centre: Safeguarding patients and nursing staff, The Finnish Patient Insurance Centre (pvk.fi), 19 Sep. 2022.
74. Potilasvakuutuskeskus: Vuosiraportti 2020, Potilasvakuutuskeskus Vuosiraportti 2020 (pvk.fi), 19 Sep. 2022.

similar action performed on the patient, or the failure to do so. The term 'other similar action' refers to, for example, a vaccination and blood or organ donation. An injury caused by an erroneous prescription or dosage of drugs may also be compensated as a treatment injury. A prerequisite for compensation is that an experienced medical professional would have performed a different procedure in the examination or treatment situation in question, thereby avoiding the injury. Consequently, a treatment injury may be, for example, a post-operative complication, such as a nerve injury or a delay in diagnosis, which could have been avoided by an experienced professional. The content and level of proficiency required from experienced healthcare personnel in Finland varies in relation to the treatment situation. For example, a general practitioner at a healthcare centre and a specialist at a university hospital have different requirements for their skills.

184. An *infection injury* refers to infections, which the patient has probably contracted in connection with an examination, treatment or other similar action. Unlike treatment injuries, infection injuries can be compensated for without determining whether the infection could have been avoided by acting differently. Many treatment procedures carry some risk of infection, and the risks are hard to avoid. In practice, this means that ordinary, superficial, fast healing infections will fall outside the scope of compensation. The compensability of the injury is decided based on a separate 'infection tolerance evaluation'. This evaluation considers the infection risk in each individual case. The infection risk comprises the risk related to the procedure and possible underlying conditions, injuries or medication of the patient that may contribute to the elevated risk. Moreover, the evaluation will consider the severity of the injury caused by the infection, the nature of the illness or injury being treated, as well as the overall health of the patient. The patient is expected to tolerate more serious consequences of an infection, the more serious the original illness or injury was that resulted in the infection and the higher the risk of infection. Yet, despite the increased risk, an injury caused by an infection may be compensable if it is rare and sudden.

185. The term *accidental injury* in the Patient Insurance Act refers to various sudden, unexpected and external events occurring without the will of the injured party and causing injury in connection with a medical examination or treatment. Accidents that occurred during patient transport by ambulance are classified as accidental injuries, unless the injury is compensable under motor liability insurance. The patient insurance only covers accident risks directly related to the procedures but not accident risks that are part of ordinary life. For example, a bodily injury suffered by a patient falling off the examination table may be a compensable accidental injury, whereas an injury that results from falling down in a hospital corridor is not an accident that is connected to treatment. However, it may be compensable as a treatment injury, if the proper patient monitoring or assistance were neglected even though it could have been provided, considering the available resources.

186. Compensation from the Patient Insurance Act can also be paid for an *equipment-related bodily injury* if the injury was caused to the patient by a defect in the equipment or device that was used for the examination, treatment, or other similar action. Such equipment or devices include surgical instruments, patient monitoring equipment and examination tables. A defect refers to any situation where a piece of equipment does not function the way it should, and the defect is not caused by the actions of the medical staff. Internal devices permanently installed in the patient, such as joint endoprostheses or pacemakers, do not qualify for compensation if defective. Compensation for these *injuries caused by permanently installed internal devices* can be applied for under the Tort Liability Act or the Product Liability Act. However, from 1 January 2021 onwards, compensation can also be paid from patient insurance for a lack in safety of a medical device permanently installed in a patient. Patient insurance pays compensation, if the medical device permanently installed in the patient in a healthcare unit is not as safe as it can be expected to be and causes a personal injury to its carrier. The time, when the device was released on the market, the foreseeable level of use of the device and other factors are taken into consideration when assessing the safety of the installed device.

187. Also, *Injury arising from damage to premises or treatment equipment* may be compensated for as a patient injury. This kind of injury may be caused e.g., by a fire. To qualify for compensation, this injury must have been sudden by nature.

188. The patient insurance covers bodily injuries caused by prescription pharmaceuticals if these drugs were delivered by the pharmacist contrary to the prescription or regulations governing the delivery of pharmaceuticals. In the most common cases, the pharmaceutical delivered or the dosage or user instructions differ from what was originally prescribed. This provision refers only to *the incorrect delivery of prescription pharmaceuticals* from the pharmacist. In other cases, injuries related pharmaceuticals being administered to the patient in conjunction with an examination or treatment are processed under treatment injuries. In that case, the compensation under patient insurance requires that the mistake be made in prescribing or dosing the medicine, judged against the standards of an experienced medical professional.

189. Side effects from pharmaceuticals which were appropriately prescribed and dosed are not compensated for under Patient Insurance. Such consequences may be compensable under voluntary Pharmaceutical Injuries Insurance.

190. If, in conjunction with appropriate examination, treatment or other corresponding processing, a severe injury occurs that is materially disproportionate with the initial situation, it may be compensated for based on the provision related to *unreasonable injury* regardless of whether the injury could have been prevented by acting in a different manner. The compensability of an injury will be decided on the basis of an unreasonableness assessment. This evaluation gives justifiable grounds for compensation only in cases where the patient has been caused a permanent severe illness, injury, or loss of life. When assessing the possible unreasonableness of an injury, the following factors will be taken into consideration: the severity of the additional injury caused by treatment, the nature and severity of the illness or injury examined or treated, the patient's overall health, the rarity of the injury and the likelihood of the injury in the individual case in question. An injury might be compensable as unreasonable if there is considerable disproportion between the consequence and the patient's illness or injury originally treated and the patient's overall health. The greater the disproportion and the greater the negative effect on the patient's health caused, the more evident it seems that the injury might be unreasonable. For example, a severely debilitating permanent neuropathic pain caused by a routine procedure might be compensable based on the unreasonableness provision. The continuation and worsening of an underlying condition are not taken into account; instead, unreasonable damage must be caused by the treatment provided. However, even severe complications are not compensated for if the risks were foreseeable by medical experts. An injury is also not compensated as unreasonable, if the injury occurs in relation to treatment administered to treat a condition that, if left untreated, could lead to the death or serious disablement of the patient.

191. Not all adverse events that occur in connection with medical treatment and healthcare are compensated in the Finnish patient insurance system. Most negative decisions are due to the fact that the injury could not be avoided despite fully appropriate treatment. For example, it is not always possible to achieve satisfactory treatment results due to the severity of the illness or injury. Such consequences are not eligible for compensation if the actions taken were in line with the standards required of an experienced medical professional, and yet the injury could not be avoided. Such an injury may, however, become compensable as an unreasonable injury in cases where the injury is sustained as a severe and sudden consequence of the treatment given.

192. Even if a sufficient level of competence is not always achieved by a medical professional, this does not necessarily mean that a patient will incur a compensable bodily injury as a result. For example, a correct diagnosis is occasionally reached only after some delay, even though proper examinations could have enabled an earlier diagnosis. The injury is not compensable if the delay had no effect on the content, prognosis or outcome of the treatment.

193. In the established practice of the Patient Insurance Centre, the following will not be compensated:

- Material damages, such as torn clothing or the loss of dentures. In these instances, the claimant may claim damages from the tortfeasor under the Tort Liability Act.
- Purely financial losses. This refers to economic loss that is not connected to bodily injury or material damage.
- Injuries occurring during ordinary social assistance services (e.g., home care) are not regarded as medical treatment and healthcare. Likewise, treatment and assistance and monitoring services connected to living in a residential care home are not covered by patient insurance.
- Insignificant injuries, even if they qualify for compensation on other grounds. An injury is considered insignificant if it causes the patient only slight pain and suffering, no permanent functional disability, no aesthetic injury, or the costs incurred do not exceed EUR 200 .

194. On an average, just over a quarter of the reported injuries are compensable. These cases are transferred to the claims assessors who will take care of the procedures for paying the compensation.

195. There is also a voluntary system in Finland that covers the injuries related to pharmaceuticals. The Pharmaceutical Injuries Insurance covers injuries that users suffer from the side effects of drugs that have been supplied for consumption in Finland.[75]

196. Pharmaceutical Injuries Insurance protects the users of pharmaceutical products. It has been taken by the Finnish Co-operative for Pharmaceutical Injury Indemnities, an organization of manufacturers, importers, distributors, or sellers of pharmaceutical products in Finland. Pharmaceutical insurance covers both pharmaceuticals released for consumption and the products that have been used in clinical trials of pharmaceutical products. It also covers the injuries caused by donated blood or by blood products.

197. Pharmaceutical injury in this insurance refers to any physical illness or injury or mental disorder that was probably caused by a pharmaceutical product. Pharmaceutical insurance does not cover small injuries. Compensation is payable if, because of the injury, the injured person has been incapable of work for an uninterrupted period of at least fourteen days or his/her bodily functions have been otherwise impaired for a period of at least fourteen days, has sustained a permanent bodily injury or illness or has died.[76]

198. All of the pharmaceutical products intended for human use that are included in section 3 of the Medicines Act (395/1987), which are distributed or obtained from Finland, are included into the Pharmaceutical Injuries Insurance, if their manufacturer, importer, marketer or seller is a member of the Finnish Co-Operative for Pharmaceutical Injury Indemnities. This means that the insurance covers nearly all pharmaceutical products sold in Finland. The beneficiary in the insurance is the end user of the pharmaceutical product (i.e., the patient).

199. However, no compensation is payable in respect of a pharmaceutical injury, if the illness or injury results from a medically inevitable risk inherent in the treatment of an illness or injury that, left untreated, would be mortal or might cause severe bodily injury. Neither is any compensation payable for such injury, or the part of it caused by the pharmaceutical, as should reasonably have been tolerated as an adverse effect of the pharmaceutical involved, taking into account the nature and severity of the illness treated, the health of the injured person; the extent of the

75. The Finnish Mutual Insurance Company for Pharmaceutical Injury Indemnities: Insurance coverage for users of medicinal products, Front page – Suomen Keskinäinen Lääkevahinkovakuutusyhtiö (laakevahinko.fi), 19 Sep. 2022.

76. The Finnish Mutual Insurance Company for Pharmaceutical Injury Indemnities: Terms and conditions, Terms and conditions – Suomen Keskinäinen Lääkevahinkovakuutusyhtiö (laakevahinko.fi) 19 Sep. 20200.

injury; the opportunities available to an expert to foresee the effect of the pharmaceutical and other similar factors. Neither is compensation payable for a pharmaceutical injury if the pharmaceutical has been used or supplied, with the user's knowledge, in a manner contrary to the provisions concerning the sale or possession of pharmaceuticals. Furthermore, no compensation is payable if the injury has been deliberately caused by the user by him/herself. Compensation for a pharmaceutical injury may be reduced or refused, if the user has through an obvious misuse of the pharmaceutical or otherwise, contributed to the injury by gross negligence.

200. If a medical device permanently installed in the patient in a healthcare unit is not as safe as it can be expected to be and causes a personal injury to its carrier, the injured party can be compensated under the Patient Insurance Act. The time when the device was released on the market, the foreseeable level of use of the device and other factors are considered when assessing the device's safety.[77] The device, however, must be installed on or after 1 January 2021. Compensation for defects and issues with safety for devices installed before this date should be sought from the manufacturer in accordance with the Product Liability Act.

201. The most common medical devices that are installed permanently in the patient are artificial joints, pacemakers, materials used to fix bone fractures, and different kinds of implants. The devices are installed in a patient with a surgical procedure or by another medical method, and they are intended to be left in place permanently or for a longer period after the procedure. A device is permanently installed if part of it is external to the body or when some part of it can be replaced only by undergoing a new procedure. The definition of permanently installed device includes also a device that releases medical substances in the person's body.

202. The Patient Insurance Act does not include medical devices intended for short-term use or that are easily detachable. Such devices include removable or dissolvable materials used to close wounds, external hearing devices, teeth alignment devices, or removable dental prostheses, prosthetic limbs or orthopaedic supports.

203. Medical devices should be safe to use from the beginning. They must be appropriate for their intended purpose and, if used properly, they should fulfil their functionality and the level of performance. If a device does not meet these requirements and the device causes a personal injury, compensation can be obtained from patient insurance.

204. The device is not considered safe if it clearly falls short of its intended life span. When assessing the requirements for the adequation service duration of a device, the patient's state of health and other characteristics as well as the expected level use for the device are taken into consideration. For example, the life span of a very active person's joint prosthetic may be shorter than the life span of a similar

77. Patient Insurance Centre: Accidents relating to permanently installed medical devices, Accidents relating to permanently instaled medical devices (pvk.fi), 19 Sep. 2022.

joint prosthetic installed in a less active person. However, a device is not considered defective solely on the grounds that a device with better features has entered the markets after the installation of a device.

205. Patient injury insurance pays compensation for the patient on the personal injuries caused by a device that is defective in terms of safety. This compensation, however, is not intended to remain in the expenses of the patient insurance system and the healthcare providers. Instead, the Patient Insurance Centre has the right to claim back the expenses from the manufacturer, importer or marketer of the device. The final compensation liability remains with the manufacturer of the device.

206. The claim for damages must according to section 31 of the Act be made to the Patient Insurance Centre within three years after the patient has learned of should have learned to know on the injury. In all cases the claim has to be made within 10 years after the incident which caused the injury.

II. Criminal Liability

207. According to section 118 of the Finnish constitution, all public officers are liable for breaches carried out in their service. Thus, they can face criminal prosecution or be obliged to pay indemnities for those who have suffered loses. Since most medical doctors in Finland are in public service, the regulation in the constitution is forming the basis for their professional liability. However, criminal proceedings against doctors are not very common in Finland. The Finnish tradition is more for complaints to the supervisory authority (Valvira) that can then restrict the professional rights of a doctor on the basis of severe or repeated mistakes.

208. However, physicians may face criminal liability either as a private practitioner or as public official. The Finish Criminal Code contains a specific Chapter 40 for the misconduct of an official. However, the liability for an injury or unlawful death is the same in both categories.

209. In the case of injury, the physician may get charged for negligent bodily injury (Chapter 21, section 10 of the Criminal Code). This crime may be fulfilled, if a person through negligence inflicts bodily injury or illness that is not insignificant on another person. The punishment for the crime is fine or imprisonment for at most six months. The key issue in checking the criteria of a crime is, whether the physician in question has followed the professional standard or not. If good professional standard was not followed and the actions of the physician increased the likelihood of an injury, the crime may have taken place, when the injury is realized.[78] However, deviation from the professional standard is not a crime for the physician as such. The physicians in Finland have large professional autonomy to select the appropriate examinations and treatments. They must, however, be able to medically justify their actions.

78. Nuutila, A: Rikosoikeudellinen huolimattomuus. Jyväskylä1996.

210. If the patient dies through the negligent actions of the physician, the physician may face charges for negligent homicide (Chapter 21, section 8 of the Criminal Code). The punishment for negligent homicide is either fine or imprisonment for at most two years. As for negligent professional injury, in negligent homicide the standard of the treatment is compared to good professional standard. Usually, courts ask the National Supervisory Authority for Welfare and Health (Valvira) to give its expert opinion whether good professional standard was followed or not. Valvira may for its statement ask opinions from various specialists. Thus, in practice the medical community has a major impact on the way how the professional standard is defined in the cases of criminal liability.

211. In the cases of gross negligence, the punishments for bodily injury or homicide can be aggravated. The punishment for grossly negligent homicide is imprisonment for at least four months and at most six years.

212. Most Finnish physicians work in public office. Primary healthcare in health centres and secondary care in hospitals is a public task. Therefore, also the regulations on offences in office (Chapter 40 in the Criminal Code) are applied to them. Most commonly, the physician may be charged for the violation of official duty. This may happen when a public official, when acting in his or her office intentionally in a manner of negligence violates his or her official duty based on the provisions or regulations to be followed in official functions. Petty violations, however, are not considered as a crime. The possible punishment for violation of official duty is fine or imprisonment for at most one year. The public official may also be sentenced to dismissal if he or she continuously or essentially is acting in violation of his or her official duties, and the offence indicates that he or she is manifestly unfit for his or her duties. Negligent violation has a less stringent punishment since negligent violation of official duties is punished with warning or fine only.

213. One rather common form of criminal offence is the breach of confidentiality. According to section 1 of Chapter 38 in the Criminal Code, a person who in violation of a secrecy duty discloses information, which should be kept secret and which he or she has learnt by virtue of his or her position or task or in the performance of a duty, or makes use of such a secret for the gain of himself or herself or another, shall be sentenced to a fine or to imprisonment for at most one year. The confidentiality may be breached not just by disclosing the secret information to outsiders, but also by utilizing the confidential information inappropriately. In addition of the secrecy offence mentioned above, public officials may also be responsible for a breach or negligent breach of official secrecy. This may take place by disclosing a document (like health records) to outsiders or by utilizing the contents of the secret document inappropriately to benefit oneself or somebody else or to harm somebody. The breach of official secrecy is punished with fine or imprisonment for at most two years. A public official may also be sentenced to dismissal if the offence demonstrates that he or she is manifestly unfit for his or her duties.

III. Vicarious Liability

214. The Finnish Tort Liability Act (412/1974) makes the employers responsible for the damages caused by their staff. The general rule, as stated in section 1 of the Chapter 3 of the Tort Liability Act, is that an employer shall be vicariously liable for damages for injury or damage caused by an employee through an error or negligence at work. The provisions on an employer apply correspondingly to the state, a municipality and another public corporation or institution, where the injury or damage has arisen through an error or negligence on the part of an employee of the public corporation, a public official or a person in a comparable service relationship.

215. Furthermore, a public corporation (like municipality, hospital district or region) shall be vicariously liable for damages for injury or damage caused through an error or negligence in the exercise of public authority. However, the liability of the public corporation arises only, if the performance of the activity or task, in view of its nature and purpose, has not met the reasonable requirements set for it. This later requirement restricts the liability of the public corporation considerably. Furthermore, if the person, who has suffered injury or damage owing to an erroneous decision by a state or municipal authority, has without an acceptable reason failed to appeal against the said decision, he/she shall not be entitled to damages from the state or the municipality for injury or damage that could have been avoided by appealing.

216. However, despite the general vicarious liability of the employer, an employee shall be liable for damages of an injury or for damages caused by him/her through an error or omission at work to an amount deemed reasonable in view of the extent of the injury or damage, the nature of the act, the status of the person causing the injury or damage, the needs of the person suffering the same, and other circumstances. If the negligence of the employee has been merely slight, he/she shall not be rendered liable for damages. If the injury or damage has been caused deliberately, full damages shall be awarded, unless it is deemed that there are special reasons for reducing the damages.

§2. Quality Assurance

217. Healthcare Act (1326/2010) has regulations concerning the quality assurance in public healthcare. Section 8 of the Healthcare Act requires that a healthcare unit must draft a separate plan about the quality management and about how patient safety is secured in the unit. Healthcare services must in all parts be based on good treatment procedures. The objectives of increased patient participation have been included into the legislation on patient safety. The Ministry of Social Affairs and Health has issued a separate decree on the contents of the plan. According to the Decree on Patient Safety Plan 341/2011, patients must be involved with patient safety work. The Healthcare Act also obliges the primary healthcare and specialized medical care to co-operate in the arrangement of a treatment of a single patient. In the case of serious illnesses or long-term illnesses, the treatment must be based on a treatment plan made together with the patient in question. Section 2 of the decree stipulates that at least the following must be included in the plan:

(1) the people in charge of and who work with quality management and patient safety and how the management will ensure that the necessary tools and resources are given to produce healthcare services that are of high-quality and safe to patients;
(2) principles and procedures of personnel management that support high-quality and safe operations and the values and procedures that support open safety culture;
(3) procedures with which the staff participates in the development of multi-professional quality management and patient safety, and with which the staff receives feedback in order to learn and develop their own skills;
(4) orientation of the staff that is required in order to produce high-quality and safe healthcare services and the education and guiding of students working in the healthcare units;
(5) procedures with which a patient and those who are close to him/her can give feedback about the flaws in quality management and inpatient safety, and procedures with which patient and person who is close to him/her are given information and support after what the patient has gone through;
(6) documents of quality management that are used in operations;
(7) the anticipation of safety and quality issues and the recognition and control of safety risks;
(8) the recognition and reporting of dangerous situations, how they are put on treatment notification system and other reporting required in legislation, and procedures done to correct the situation; and
(9) the co-operation needed to ensure quality management and patient safety with other healthcare units of the hospital district.

218. In addition, the plan must include the necessary availability of the services, treatment-chains, the physical environment of the healthcare unit, infections that are common in healthcare, medical treatment and the organizing of medicinal service, equipment and tools used in healthcare, staff, how the tasks are divided between them and what are their skills, information systems and how patient documents are drafted, and how information is passed within healthcare unit and between healthcare units.

219. A private healthcare services provider should also have a plan to ensure quality management and patient safety even though Private Healthcare Act doesn't directly require it. However, the provider of private healthcare services must make a plan for the supervision of the services to follow any issues that might affect patient safety. If the service provider operates in two or more locations, the director in charge of healthcare must draft a written plan that covers the service provider and its offices in different locations to ensure quality management.

220. The plan for the supervision of services includes all actions with what the healthcare service providers supervise their own actions, its quality and the performance of staff and services it provides. All different operational and procedural guidelines that are given to ensure uniform procedures in the services.

221. National Supervisory Authority for Welfare and Health has given a decree (2/2012) about the detailed contents of the plan.[79] According to the decree, the service provider must always draft a plan before starting the operations. The plan must be delivered to licensing authority at latest with the start-up notification. The plan must include information about the service provider and the locations of the offices. In addition, it must describe the organization of the supervision and the duties of director in charge of healthcare services. Finally, the plan must describe the operations, quality management, risk recognition and actions for corrective measures.

222. The recognition of high-risk operations, supervision, evaluation and informing of dangerous situations must be emphasized in the risk analysis included in the plan. The staff must be aware of the necessary procedures taken in dangerous situations.

223. Possible exceptions from the approved practices and procedures done in the operations must be documented and handled properly. The instructions regarding the handling of exceptions must include the handling process with involved procedures, responsibilities and correction measures. The effects of exceptions to patient safety must also always be evaluated.

224. The plan for the supervision of services must include the description of the amount and structure of staff. Furthermore, the description of the required updating and additional training to supplement the knowledge and education of the staff must be described.

225. The employer is in charge of checking that the work applicant has the competence to perform the tasks required in healthcare, including sufficient language skills. This means that the employer must check the applicant's competence from diplomas and from the Register of Healthcare Professionals.

226. Procedures used to supervise the staff's actions, notes made to patient documents and prescription practices must be included in the plan.

227. Furthermore, a description of office spaces used in private healthcare services must be added into the plan. For the spaces critical for patient safety (including treatment and operating rooms), the designs, space requirements and their suitability for their purpose of use must be described. Special attention must be paid to proper organization of medicine maintenance rooms and of laboratories, to access control of healthcare spaces and to burglary and fire protection.

---

79. Sosiaali- ja terveydenhuollon lupa ja valvontavirasto: Omavalvontasuunnitelma, Omavalvontasuunnitelma – Valvira, 20 Sep. 2022.

228. If a healthcare service provider operates on the premises owned by another healthcare service provider, they must draft a plan which shows how the healthcare service provider acting as leaser and the healthcare service provider acting as tenant have agreed on operations including the spaces, equipment and materials needed in healthcare, hygiene practices and the administration of patient documents. Section 4 of the Private Healthcare Decree stipulates that the license application must include an auditor's report about the spaces and equipment, and ambulance and its equipment, signed by a responsible physician or responsible dentist. A copy of this report must be attached to the plan on the supervision of the services.

§3. Review Boards

229. There are regional ethics committees Institutional Review Boards (IRB) in each of the five University Hospitals in Finland as well as one (TUKIJA) in the national level.[80] The section 4 of the Act on Medical Research (488/1999) requires that the benefit and wellbeing of the research subject is placed above the interests of science and society. The investigator should try to prevent any predictable risks and harms to the research subject. He may be exposed only to such interventions that may produce greater health or scientific benefits than are the anticipated risks and harms. In addition to the investigator, also the IRB should take these into the consideration, when giving its opinion. It should be emphasized that the research subject cannot give valid consent to research where these requirements are not fulfilled.

230. The research in embryo and human foetus falls under the Act on Medical Research. Prior to the initiation of any research intervention, the investigator has to evaluate the potential risks and harms for the research subjects. Those must be compared with the expected benefits for the patients or other subjects. Section 3 of the Act requires that an independent research ethics board (IRB) has given a favourable opinion on the research protocol. If the research protocol is revised in substantial parts, the IRB has to evaluate the change.

§4. Disciplinary Organizations

231. According to section 1 of the Act on Healthcare Professionals, the National Supervisory Authority for Welfare and Health (Valvira) is responsible for the national guidance and supervision of healthcare professionals. Furthermore, regionally the activities of healthcare professionals are guided and supervised by Regional State Administrative Agencies in their area. The National Supervisory Authority for Welfare and Health deals with the matters related to the guidance and supervision of healthcare professionals especially in questions concerning:

80. Tukija: National Committee on Medical Research Ethics (Tukija), Tukija.fi – Frontpage – tukija englanti, 20 Sep. 2022.

(1) matters that are important as a matter of principle or otherwise have far-reaching impacts;
(2) a suspicion of medical malpractice that has caused the death or a person or a difficult permanent disability to a person;
(3) matters that are related to investigation of the cause of death carried out by a medicolegal expert;
(4) matters that may require precautionary or disciplinary measures; or
(5) matters that the relevant Regional State Administrative Agency is disqualified to handle.

232. For the supervision of healthcare professionals, the National Supervisory Authority for Welfare and Health has established a Board for the Supervision of Healthcare Professionals, the composition and tasks of which are prescribed by specific Government decree (1550/2009).

233. The supervisory authority does not take into consideration a complaint related to the activity of a healthcare professional that concerns a matter that took place more than five years ago, unless there are particular grounds for considering the complaint.

234. If there is good reason to presume that a healthcare professional, owing to illness, substance abuse, reduced functional capacity or for equivalent reason, is no longer capable of practicing his or her profession, the National Supervisory Authority for Welfare and Health may according to section 25 of the Act on Healthcare Professionals order the healthcare professional to undergo a medical examination or examinations at a hospital (examination of capacity for professional activity and state of health). If there are good reasons to presume that the professional skills or knowledge of a healthcare professional are inadequate, the National Supervisory Authority for Welfare and Health may order the healthcare professional to have an examination, to demonstrate skills or to undergo an investigation in order to get his or her professional skills or knowledge assessed (investigation of professional skills).

235. The National Supervisory Authority for Welfare and Health may issue sanctions to healthcare professionals for misconduct, if a healthcare professional neglects any obligation of the Act on Healthcare Professionals or performs tasks for which his or her training and professional skills and knowledge shall be considered inadequate or his or her opportunities for action limited, or acts otherwise incorrectly or reprehensibly. The National Supervisory Authority for Welfare and Health may, in the cases listed above issue to the person specific regulations and instructions for professional activity, impose restrictions on the right to practice professional activity as a licensed professional for a fixed period or until further notice, withdraw the right to practice the profession of a licensed professional for a fixed time or until further notice, prohibit a professional with a protected title to use the occupational title of a healthcare professional as prescribed by decree for a fixed period or until further notice or cancel the right of a licensed professional to practice his or her profession. The National Supervisory Authority for Welfare and

Health or the Regional State Administrative Agency may also give the healthcare professional an admonition or draw his or her attention to appropriate professional practice. The admonition issued or the drawing of attention by the National Supervisory Authority for Welfare and Health or the Regional State Administrative Agency referred to in this section may not be appealed.

236. If a healthcare professional has been sentenced to imprisonment for a criminal offence that he or she has committed while carrying on professional activity, and the decision of the court has become legally binding, and if the circumstances relating to the offence show that he or she is not worthy of the confidence he or she should enjoy, the National Supervisory Authority for Welfare and Health may withdraw the right to practice a profession of a licensed professional for a fixed period or, under aggravating circumstances, permanently, or cancel the authorization of an authorized professional for a fixed period or, under aggravating circumstances, permanently, or forbid a professional with a protected occupational title to use the occupational title of a healthcare professional as provided by decree for a fixed period or, under aggravating circumstances, permanently.[81] If a healthcare professional holding a state or municipal office or an office in a joint municipal board has been ordered to be suspended from office or dismissed from office because of a criminal offence, the provisions in section 1 above shall apply, correspondingly. The court shall send copies of the record and decision concerning the case to the National Supervisory Authority for Welfare and Health without delay.

---

81. National Supervisory Authority for Welfare and Health, Record number 1/05.01.03.02/2010: The license of a nurse, who had stolen morphine-ampoules from his workplace, was removed after he didn't take the actions the Authority required to get control of his substance issues, which he had previously admitted; and National Supervisory Authority for Welfare and Health, Record number 915/05.01.03.00/2009 and 1259/09/900/08: The pharmacy informed the Authority of a physician, who prescribed great amounts of Temgesic-medicine to his patients regardless of previous deliveries. On the basis of prescription account the Authority received, it ordered the physician in question to deliver patient documents of eight different patients and give an account of treatment he had given to them. A professional opinion was also acquired. While the procedure was already pending, another pharmacy informed the Authority that the physician in question had prescribed great amounts of medicines affecting the central nervous system to people who had previously had substance issues.

The National Supervisory Authority for Welfare and Health stated that the records the doctor in question had made of his patients were very brief and usually included only scattered and imprecise information about the prescribed medicines. The objectives of the treatment, diagnosis, the basis of the treatment decisions, treatment plans and follow-up information were imperfectly or not at all put on a record. It is noteworthy that, as the prescription account showed, almost all prescriptions of CNS-medicines and of narcotics were not put on patient records.

A suspicion of seriously inappropriate and reproachable actions had occurred in this matter. On the basis of received accounts and statements, it was likely that patient safety was seriously endangered due to physician's actions. The received accounts and statements showed that due to serious patient safety risk fast intervention to physician's license was necessary even before all required information was received and a final decision on the license could be made.

Due to the abovementioned, National Supervisory Authority for Welfare and Health considered it proper to temporarily restrict the physician's license to prescribe narcotics or medicines containing buprenorphine. The temporary restriction was ordered to be in force until National Supervisory Authority for Welfare and Health had settled the matter finally.

237. In dealing with matters referred to in section 25, the National Supervisory Authority for Welfare and Health may, as necessary, temporarily forbid a licensed professional to practice a profession, or temporarily limit the right to practice a profession, or temporarily cancel the authorization of an authorized professional, or temporarily forbid a professional with a protected occupational title to use the occupational title of a healthcare professional as prescribed by decree.

238. When the right to practice as a healthcare professional has been withdrawn for a fixed period or until further notice or has been limited or denied, when the authorization to practice professional activity has been cancelled or when use of a healthcare professional occupational title as prescribed by decree has been forbidden, the healthcare professional may apply for restoration of the right to practice a profession or nullification of any limitation on professional activity, restoration of authorization to practice a profession, or restoration of right to use the occupational title of a healthcare professional.

239. If a healthcare professional has in the course of his or her professional activity violated the law or the provisions or regulations issued on the basis of it or is otherwise guilty of error or neglect in his or her duty, the error or neglect not being of a kind requiring prosecution in a court of justice, the National Supervisory Authority for Welfare and Health may issue a written admonition or warning to healthcare professional.

240. If healthcare professional is unable to act as healthcare professional due to illness, substance abuse, declined health or due to similar reason, National Supervisory Authority for Welfare and Health may decide on required actions as stipulated in section 26 of Act on Healthcare Professionals. This means usually that the right to practice profession in healthcare is either restricted or removed.[82] Most of restrictions made in right to practice profession in healthcare are made on the basis of this section due to declined health (e.g., mental health issues) or due to substance issues.

241. According to section 40 of the Act on Healthcare Professionals, the supervisory authorities have the right to have access to patient records and other relevant

82. National Supervisory Authority for Welfare and Health, Record number 960/05.01.03.00/2009: A supervision-matter was started at National Supervisory Authority for Welfare and Health by a notice, in which a physician was told to have retired over ten years ago due to health issues. Also, police had contacted the Authority about the same physician because of the physician's questionable prescription manners, especially his habit to prescribe addictive medication which affects the central nervous system. During the clearance of the matter, the prescription account showed that the physician had prescribed significant amounts of those medications for himself and to his partner. The medical statements made over ten years before showed that the physician's work ability had declined so much that he wasn't considered able to work as a physician in hospital if employer couldn't in part-time physician's work arrange various and sufficient possibilities for support, guidance and consultation. National Supervisory Authority for Welfare and Health obliged the doctor to go to medical examination to determine his medical condition. His health had declined so much that it was considered impossible for him to continue in the profession.

documents, when evaluating the appropriateness of the actions of a healthcare professional. The healthcare professionals' obligation to inform National Supervisory Authority for Welfare and Health can be criticized in the light of international human rights agreements, especially in the light of self-incrimination. Self-incrimination means that a person is forced or pressured to witness against himself when standing trial. International human rights agreements prohibit these types of actions against the accused. The idea is that the authorities can't use indiscreet actions to force oneself to give a statement that is against his best interest. Prohibition of self-incrimination isn't limited to the confession of criminal activities or to statements that clearly prove liability. The prohibition must also include statements given under pressure that are taken to prove the inconsistency between the statements the accused has made or to unbalance his credibility.[83]

242. Section 26 of the Act on Healthcare Professionals stipulates that the National Supervisory Authority for Welfare and Health may give provisions or guidelines, restrict the right to practice a profession or even remove them completely, if the healthcare professional is found guilty of incorrect actions. Healthcare professional may appeal to administrative court of the decision made by National Supervisory Authority for Welfare and Health. There are, indeed, some court cases where the decisions of the supervisory authority have been evaluated:

> The Supreme Administrative Court, 28.11.2012/3325
>
> National Supervisory Authority for Welfare and Health had restricted nurse's right to practice the profession, as stipulated in the sections 26 and 28 in Act on Healthcare Professionals, temporarily so that the nurse in question wasn't able to work in a public healthcare unit without supervision and guidance from another healthcare professional, The nurse in question wasn't also allowed to handle medicines. The basis of the restriction was that the nurse had given painkillers against instruction. Also, the workability statement about inappropriate practices, ability to function and health was used as basis for the restriction decision.
>
> Administrative court changed the restriction decision given by National Supervisory Authority for Welfare and Health to a warning as stipulated in section 33 of the Act on Healthcare Professionals.
>
> The Supreme Administrative Court overruled administrative court's decision after National Supervisory Authority for Welfare and Health had appealed on administrative court's decision and validated the decision of National Supervisory Authority for Welfare and Health. The workability showed serious concerns over the nurse's ability to function and health, and these concerns affected negatively on the nurse's possibilities to work independently and to participate in medicinal care. The decision of National Supervisory Authority for Welfare and Health was in accordance with the objective of patient safety, and thus not against the requirements of relativity. Administrative court

83. Finnish Supreme Court decision KKO:2009:80.

couldn't change a restriction meant for precautionary measures into warning, which was only a disciplinary measure.

243. Section 32 of the Act on Healthcare Professionals stipulates that healthcare professional may apply for the return of right to practice the profession after the reason of removal of rights has ended.

244. The membership in the Finnish Medical Association which is representing physicians is not a prerequisite for practising as physician in Finland, even though the membership fee also covers patient insurance fee. There are a lot of physicians in Finland who do not belong to the Finnish Medical Association that is also a trade union responsible for negotiation of terms for national agreements on salaries. For example, university professors in medical field may join to the Professors Union instead of Finnish Medical Association.[84] For its members, however, Finnish Medical Association may impose sanctions, if his/her activities are not following the principles of the association. Finnish Medical Association is specially following the marketing of medical services as well as collegiality requirements.[85] In the cases of improper marketing or conduct, the Association may impose a public warning to its member.[86]

84. Finnish Union for University Professors: Union, Union – Professoriliitto, 20 Sep. 2022.
85. Lääkäriliitto: Kollegiaalisuusohjeet, Lääkäriliitto – Kollegiaalisuusohjeet (laakariliitto.fi), 20 Sep. 2022.
86. Lääkäriliitto: Lääkäreitä ja lääkärinpalveluja koskevat markkinointiohjeet, Lääkäriliitto – Lääkäreitä ja lääkärinpalveluja koskevat markkinointiohjeet (laakariliitto.fi), 20 Sep. 2022.

Part II. The Physician: Patient Relationship

Chapter 1. General Description

§1. Rights and Duties of Physicians and Patients

245. The rights of the patients in healthcare were a major topic in health policy discussion in Finland in late 1970s. The discussion resulted in parliamentary committee drafting the legislation for the compensation of medical injuries as well of the requirements for consent to treatment. The Act on the Status and Rights of Patients (785/1992, the Patient's Rights Act) was a result of some 10 years of preparation. It includes regulations concerning consent and privacy of the patient, as well as regulations on minor and incapacitated patients. Finland was the first country in the world to have specific legislation on the rights or the patients.

246. The Patient's Rights Act is applied to all healthcare and medical care (i.e., both public and private units) in Finland. The Act applies to everyone regardless of the nature of the illness or the patient's age.[87] However, the Act is secondary to other legislation. This means that when other legislation has e.g., regulations on the compulsory treatment of a patient (the Act on Metal Care), Patient's Rights Act is applied only to the extent that the activities are not covered by other legislation.

247. Section 2 of the Patient's Rights Act defines some key concepts. The term patient is used of a person who uses healthcare services or is otherwise an object of them. Furthermore, the terms healthcare and medical care in the Act mean measures taken by healthcare professionals or in a healthcare unit in order to assess the state of health of a person or to restore or maintain it. The term healthcare professionals indicate persons referred to in section 2 of the Act on Healthcare Professionals.

§2. Informed Consent

248. The right to self-determination is a key concept in the human rights treaties and fundamental rights ratified by Finland. It is also the right on which several other rights are built on. The right to self-determination is a basic concept that includes, firstly, the right to liberty and equality and the prohibition of discrimination. Secondly, it includes the right to privacy and personal integrity, and thirdly, the right to

87. Lohiniva-Kerkelä M, Potilaan oikeudet, in Terveysoikeus, p. 160, Talentum 2015.

competence. The right to self-determination is guaranteed under section 7 of the Finnish Constitution as part of the right to life, personal liberty and integrity. It is also closely linked to the protection of privacy (section 10), which includes the right to determine oneself and one's body. In the European Convention on Human Rights, the right to self-determination is linked to the right to liberty and security enshrined in Article 5.[88]

249. Every patient-doctor relationship is a matter of patient's integrity and interference, as well as respect for the patient as a subject. The patient's right to self-determination is exercised as consent to treatment or research in accordance with the informed consent doctrine. Respect for the right to self-determination must be obeyed as far as possible. Legally, the doctor decides whether to take the patient for treatment and how to treat the patient. The doctor's right is limited by the patient's right to consent and refuse treatment. This means that the patient or his/her representatives also take part to decisions on treatment. An exception to this is the decisions on involuntary treatment of psychiatric patients.[89]

250. Section 6 of the Patient's Rights Act requires that the method of treatment must be based on mutual understanding between the patient and healthcare personnel. If the patient refuses a specified treatment or measure, he/she should be treated in another medically acceptable way. In some cases, there is a possibility for involuntary treatment. These cases are listed in the Mental Health Act (1116/1990), the Communicable Diseases Act (1227/2016) and the Substance Abuse Act (41/1986) and in Child Welfare Act (417/2007). The decision to treat the patient without his or her consent must always be considered inherently.

251. The Patient's Rights Act does not, however, specify how the patient shall give consent and therefore it must be judged on a case-by-case basis taking into account the nature of the treatment, the extent to which the integrity of the person is compromised and the specific circumstances.[90] The exercise of the right to self-determination presupposes a person's competence, which means the ability to understand the meaning of treatment or refusal of treatment and its health effects. According to the general principles of law, voluntary, non-coercive opinion-forming and decision-making are the starting points for this. It is, however, important to note that the patient is not required to have legal capacity.[91] The key is that he or she can understand aspects that are adequate for treatment and research. The doctor will decide if the patient can make decisions concerning his treatment.

252. The patient's consent can be explicit or tacit, and in deciding which type of consent is needed, the nature of the treatment is assessed. The preparatory works of

88. Government proposal, 309/1993 vp. and Irma Pahlman, Potilaan itsemääräämisoikeus, Edita Publishing Oy 2003, pp. 182–183.
89. Lohiniva-Kerkelä M: Potilaan oikeudet, in Terveysoikeus, p. 194, Talentum 2015.
90. Lohiniva-Kerkelä M: Potilaan oikeudet, in Terveysoikeus 2015, p. 196.
91. Nordic Legal Research Group on Health Law: Patient's consent to treatment – a Nordic perspective on medical self–determination, Report from Finland, Nordic_LRG_Medical_Law.pdf (elsa.org), 16 Oct. 2022.

the Patient's Rights Act provide unclear information considering this distinction: On the one hand, they state that consent can be tacit in situations where the patient is treated for a minor sub-measure of treatment, and on the other hand they imply that the treatment itself must be minor.[92] The more there are treatment options and the more serious the issue of patient integrity is, the more important it is to ensure explicit consent. Such consent may be either oral or written. When it is apparent for the patient to know what a routine treatment contains and the mentioned treatment is non-invasive, explicit consent is not necessary. In this case, the patient's tacit consent is detectable from their behaviour.

253. Oral consent helps to prevent the excessive bureaucratization of healthcare, and it is generally the most efficient way of giving explicit consent.[93] The demarcation between oral and tacit consent is not always clear, and, for example, a nod of the head is construed conceptually as oral consent despite its non-verbality. Oral consent can be seen as the standard form of the patient's consent in Finland and it functions in situations which are more serious than minor procedures allowing a tacit consent, but not serious and possibly arguable enough in order to require written consent. There are a few cases, however, where it is necessary to obtain a written consent from the patient. These include acting as a donor in solid organ transplantation or a donor of gem cells for in vitro fertilization purposes. Furthermore, written consent is also required from the research subjects in medical research.[94] Even if the consent not being provided in a written form, the relevant information concerning the treatments and examinations should be recorded in the patient journals.

254. A patient may refuse at any stage the treatment or procedure planned for him, including treatments that have already started. He can also agree to treatment after consideration, even if he had initially refused it. Section 6 of the Patient's Rights Act also states that if a patient refuses a certain treatment or measure, he has to be cared for, as far as possible, in another medically acceptable way in mutual understanding with him. The patient also has the right to make decisions that may harm his or her own health or life and has the right to refuse treatment planned or already started to him, and those involved in patient care must respect the decisions of the patient.[95] However, the decision to implement treatment is always made by a healthcare professional and while the patient has the right to refuse the proposed treatment, he/she will also have the responsibility for his/her own decisions, when the treatment is continued in another medically acceptable way. The right to refuse treatment also applies to situations which result in the patient's death, serious injury, serious illness or risk of such illness.[96]

---

92. Government proposal 185/1991, p. 16.
93. Salla Lötjönen, 'Loukatun suostumuksesta potilaan itsemääräämisoikeuteen' Lakimies 7–8/2004, pp. 1398–1420.
94. Lötjönen, Salla: Lääketieteellinen tutkimus ihmisillä. Oikeudellisia ja eettisiä näkökohtia ruumiilliseen koskemattomuuteen puuttumisesta lääketieteellisessä tutkimuksessa. Helsinki 2004.
95. Valvira: Potilaan itsemääräämisoikeus, Potilaan itsemääräämisoikeus – Valvira, 25 Sep. 2022.
96. Pahlman I, Potilaan itsemääräämisoikeus, in Terveysoikeus, Talentum 2014, p. 194.

255. Although a patient cannot be left untreated because of a refusal, the patient is not entitled to require a particular type of treatment. The doctor decides on the treatment in accordance with section 22 of the Act on Healthcare Professionals (559/1994). The same goes for medical research, where the responsible physician supervises and decides on the patient's examinations. Even in these situations, the patient always has the right to refuse the treatment that has been provided by a doctor.

256. The mutual understanding on appropriate treatment must be based on adequate information. Section 5 of the Act states that 'a patient shall be given information about their state of health, the significance of the treatment, various alternative forms of treatment and their effects as well as about other factors related to their treatment that are significant when decisions are made on the treatment given to them'. The purpose of providing information is essentially to guarantee that the patient can consider whether to consent to a particular treatment or not. The list of the information to be provided continues in the law drafting material, where it is specified that before beginning any treatment, an explanation of the treatment's extent, risk factors, complications, likelihood of failure and what would happen, if the treatment is waived, shall be disclosed to the patient.

257. The obligation to inform lies by the healthcare professionals. Although the right to be informed is a derivative of the patient's self-determination, it also has an important role in promoting trust between the healthcare personnel and the patient. Therefore, healthcare professionals are required to disclose information on their own initiative.[97]

258. The healthcare professionals should give the information in such a way that the patient can understand it. Usage of professional medical language is not appropriate, if the patient cannot understand it. The scope of the required information is also shaped by the patients' right to self-determination: some patients may want to know every little detail of their treatment while others might only want to know the bare minimum or even refuse to be informed. It is noteworthy that the law does require that all available information must be explained to a patient.[98]

259. The way of information required by the Patient's Rights Act can be described as a communication-based approach, even if the healthcare professionals are obliged to take the initiative. The content of the obligation to inform takes shape during the communication process and it is decided situation-by-situation how broad or specific the provided information should be.[99] However, there are some standards for required information that have developed in the praxis of supervising

97. Government Proposal 185/1991, p. 15.
98. Lehtonen L: Mitä käytännössä tarkoittaa yhteisymmärrys hoidosta. Suomen Lääkärilehti 2004:15–16, 1685–1690.
99. Nordic Legal Research Group on Health Law: Patient's consent to treatment – a Nordic perspective on medical self-determination, Report from Finland, Nordic_LRG_Medical_Law.pdf (elsa.org), 16 Oct. 2022.

authorities also in Finland.[100] In public healthcare usually the standard of experienced professional is followed i.e., the information provided to the patient is compared to the information that an experienced physician would have given in a similar case. In private healthcare, however, the requirements for consumer protection also play a role as stipulated in section 13 of Chapter 8 of the Finnish Act on Consumer Protection (38/1978). If the service differs from the information that has been provided to the patient, the private service provider is obliged to compensates the possible damages to the patients. In practice, however, the consumer protection authorities in Finland have lined that the typical patient is receiving adequate information, if it is given in a way that an experienced professional would have given.

260. When disclosing information, the following factors must be taken into consideration: patient's age, education, native language and other characteristics of the individual.[101] In principle, mature children and persons with disabilities can exercise their right to self-determination and make autonomous decisions when certain conditions are met. Consequently, the opinion of a minor on a treatment measure has to be asked if it is feasible taking into consideration the age and level of development. But if the minor cannot understand the treatment, the treatment has to be performed in mutual understanding with their guardian or legal representative.

261. There are two exceptions to the obligation to inform: The first exception is when the patient refuses to receive information. The second exception for the obligation to inform is when it's obvious that giving the information would cause serious hazard to the life or health of the patient. This provision must be interpreted very restrictively, because it goes against the general principles of patient autonomy and the right to be informed. Thus, mere suspicion of the potential harm information disclosure might cause is not enough, the harm must be evident.[102] The main group in this category are mental patient with a risk of suicide. It is, however, also possible to provide information later, when the patient's mental state has improved.

262. There is also the possibility that the patient is not able to receive information and express his opinion (e.g., in emergencies with unconscious patient). In such cases, the patient must be given necessary treatment to protect his life and health, unless the patient has earlier steadfastly and competently expressed the refusal.

263. If a major patient because of mental disturbance, mental retardation or for other reasons cannot decide on the treatment given to him or her, the legal representative, a family member or other close person of the patient has to be heard before making an important decision concerning a treatment that would be in accordance with the patient's will. If this matter cannot be assessed, the patient must be given a treatment that can be considered to be in accordance with individuals, their personal interests as stipulated in section 6 of the Patient's Rights Act. Important

100. Rynning E: Samtycke till medicinsk vård och behandling: En rättsvetenskaplig studie. Uppsala 1994.
101. Government Proposal 185/1991, p. 15.
102. Government Proposal 185/1991, p. 15.

treatment decisions must therefore be discussed with the patient's legal representative, a close relative, or another close person. The patient's close relatives refer mainly to the spouse, children, parents and siblings. Another close relative or close person could be the patient's common-law partner or another person who has a permanent resident with the patient. Consent should take into account the previously expressed patient's will. If the patient has not expressed a will to treat, their interests should be taken into account.[103] According to section 9 of the Patient's Rights Act the guardian or other legal representative of a minor patients doesn't, however, have the right to forbid any care which may be required to avert a threat to the patient's life or health.

264. When the patient's therapeutic preferences are unknown, and cannot be resolved e.g., due to the patient's unconsciousness, the doctor is obligated to give the treatment, if deemed necessary in order to the patient's life or health. Healthcare professionals thus cannot refuse from giving necessary treatment that is medically appropriate to the patient. Emergency treatment must always be given when necessary to prevent the dangers threatening the patient's life or health, even when the patient's will cannot be clarified due to their unconsciousness or for other reasons. However, if the patient has previously stated his/her refusal, for example, through an advance directive, the doctor cannot give a treatment, which is clearly against the will of the patient.

265. There are few cases in Finish legislation, where medical interventions are compulsory. These include actions to prevent the spreading of contagious diseases and treatment of mental patients that do not have the capacity to consent for the treatment. Furthermore, there are requirements also in the Act on Occupational Healthcare on compulsory medical examinations. If the health examination made for employee shows that due to his/her personal features he/she has obvious susceptibility to endanger his/her health in the work, section 10 of Act on Occupational Healthcare stipulates that he/she cannot be used in such work. Section 13 of Act on Occupational Healthcare stipulates that employee cannot without a proper reason refuse participating in health examination stipulated in the section in question. Provisions about occupational healthcare have been legislated for the protection of employee. The obligation to participate is based on society's interest to protect the health of employees. The obligatory participation in health examinations has been justified for not leaving employer possibility to neglect his/her obligations to employee by reasoning it with employee's unwillingness.

266. The 2 item of paragraph 1 of section 13 of Act on Occupational Healthcare stipulates that compulsory health examinations can be made when an employee has normal ability to function but work is such that it has effects on health which must be cleared or when the work is ordinary but the healthcare of employee is such that it must be found out whether he/she can stand the demands of work. This means that employee can be ordered to compulsory health examination either on work or

103. Government proposal 185/1991, p. 17.

employee-based reasons. Employee can be ordered to health examination either when she/he is starting the work or when she/he is already working.

267. Emergency medical interventions form another exception on consent requirements. Section 50 of the Healthcare Act defines emergency medical treatment as 'involving an injury, a sudden onset of an illness, an exacerbation or a long-term illness, or a deterioration of functional ability where immediate intervention is required and where treatment cannot be postponed without risking or worsening the condition or further injury.' Section 8 of the Patient's Rights Act regulates emergency treatments. According to this section, 'a patient has to be given treatment necessary to prevent harm to his/her life or health even in case it is not possible to assess the patient's will because of unconsciousness or other reason'. However, if the patient has expressed their will earlier steadfastly and competently, he or she must not receive any treatment that goes against their will. Therefore, the patient's wishes must be respected in regard to emergency treatment and intensive care. Furthermore, there always must always be appropriate medical grounds for the treatment.

268. It is not in the patient's best interest to have treatment that is not medically justified. Section 8 of the Patient's Rights Act is meant to be applied in instances where the patient's wishes cannot be inquired and the need for treatment is urgent and postponing medical treatment would be harmful to the patient's health or even lead to death.[104] It is noteworthy that a suicide attempt is not considered as a refusal of treatment by the patient.

§3. Privacy

269. Section 8 of the Finnish Constitution protects everyone's right to privacy. In healthcare, the right to privacy is realized both in the protection of self-determination and in secrecy requirements.[105] The right to privacy in the Finnish Constitution resembles the Article 8 of the European Convention on Human Rights.

270. The right to privacy has several spheres. The core part of the privacy is the right to make decisions on intervention on one's own body. Intrusions without consent are a criminal offence. However, the outer spheres of privacy include to utilization of personal data as well as the protection of social contacts.[106] Especially in childcare cases, the conflict of privacy rights of a family *v.* the benefit of the child is often imminent. In the Finnish legal system, the privacy rights can be restricted by an Act of the parliament when the restrictions are deemed necessary e.g., to protect other basic rights (including the life or health of others).

104. Government Proposal 185/1991.
105. Lehtonen L, Potilaan yksityisyyden suoja, Vammala 2001.
106. Lehtonen L: Potilaan yksityisyyden suoja, Vammala 2001.

271. However, passing the information on patient's health and treatments is essential for good quality healthcare. Section 12 of the Patient's Rights Act mandates the healthcare professional to keep records on their patients. Healthcare professionals are obliged to record in patient documents the information necessary for the arranging, planning, providing and monitoring of care and treatment for a patient. Detailed provisions on the drawing up of patient documents and on keeping them as well as biological samples are issued in the Decree of the Ministry of Social Affairs and Health (94/2022).[107] The decree, however, does not provide exhaustive guidance on to what extent the relevant information gathered during examination and treatment sessions should be recorded. Since the relevant information from each patient encounter should be recorded, it seems reasonable to exercise case-by-case consideration. In most cases, a summary of the treatment or examination is sufficient to ensure good care of the patient, and in contradictory or atypical cases, a more thorough recording is needed. This view is supported by the Decree, which stipulates that the more difficult and critical the patient's situation is or the more significant the treatment decisions are, the more precise and detailed the recording to the patient journal should be.

272. Records of patient journals should adequately reflect the rationale for the diagnosis, treatment chosen, and treatment decisions made. The choice of examination and treatment methods with different effects and risks must be marked to show the reasons for the chosen method. The rationale for each procedure should be clearly defined in the patient journals. However, the Parliamentary Ombudsman has found that patient journals are often completely devoid of records of discussions with the patient about his care and the views expressed by him.[108] If the journals lack the patient's view of the treatment or care he wishes to receive for example in the future, it can have serious consequences in situations where the patient is unable to provide his view later because of a mental disturbance, intellectual disability or other similar reasons.

273. The patient's consent or refusal (either explicit or tacit) is found in the patient journals as well, since it is required to treat the patient in an agreement with him, and also document the outcomes of the relevant conversations with the patient.[109] If the patient refuses the examination or treatment, the refusal must be reliably confirmed in the patient journals.

274. An advance directive is always recorded in the patient journals and it can be given explicitly – either orally or in writing. Through the advance directive the

107. Decree of the Ministry of Social Affairs and Health on Patient Journals (94/2022) 11 §: Information on service events should include, to the extent necessary, the reason for the visit, preliminary information, current status, observations, examination findings, problems, diagnosis or health risk, conclusions, treatment planning, implementation and follow-up, disease course and final statement.
108. Oikeusasiamies Riitta-Leena Paunio: EOA Dnro 2828/2/07, Puutteelliset potilasasiakirjamerkinnät, C:\Temp\EOAE_2828_V07.RLP_TEH.pdf.pdf (oikeusasiamies.fi), 25 Sep. 2022.
109. Lääkärilehti. Soininen, M. Miten korjataan jos potilas kieltäytyy hoidosta? Available online: https://www.laakarilehti.fi/ajassa/ajankohtaista/miten-kirjaan-jos-potilas-kieltaytyy-hoidosta/, 25 Sep. 2022.

patient continues to exercise the right to self-determination even after he is unable to decide on the treatment in accordance with the Patient's Rights Act. In his advance directive, the patient may refuse life-prolonging treatment in a situation where it is likely to only prolong suffering. On the other hand, the patient can also express his wishes regarding active treatment. Refusal of hope for active treatment expressed in the advance directive is binding on the healthcare professionals and guides the decisions of the patient's relatives, unless there is a justified reason to assume that the patient's will has changed.

275. The patient records of the primary healthcare and specialized medical care within a region compose a shared patient information register. This register contains all patient records of all healthcare units regardless of how and when they were made or saved. However, the register will never contain patient information of Private Healthcare Units, not even when a municipality or federation of municipalities owns it completely. The usage of patient information for treatment doesn't require explicit consent from the patient in question. However, the patient does have a right to deny the usage of his/her patient records in another healthcare unit.

276. In Finland, it is mandatory to use electronic health records both in public and private healthcare and integrate the system to the national patient data repository Kanta, which is maintained by the Social Insurance Institution of Finland (Kela).[110] This obligation is based on the Act on Electronic Processing of Customer Information within Social and Healthcare (784/2021). Also, prescriptions in Finland are issued electronically.[111] Paper or telephone prescriptions can be issued only in exceptional cases. All prescriptions are issued and dispensed via the Kanta services.

277. The Patient Data Repository (Kanta) plays a central role in passing information between healthcare service providers. Each healthcare professional has their personal identity card to be used when logging in to the appropriate electronic health record system. They have to confirm the purpose of the use of the patient data they are searching. The patient can retrospectively check who have looked his/her records. The patient can also according to the section 18 of the Act restrict the use of his/her data, but the patient records will still be available for emergency care.[112]

278. Citizens can see the data recorded by the healthcare units in the My Kanta service. The patient records are archived in a technically uniform format, which enables the transferability of the data from one system to another and improves the accessibility of information in operational units involved in the treatment of the patient.

---

110. Kanta: Patient Data Repository, Patient Data Repository – Kanta.fi, 25 Sep. 2022.
111. Act on Electronic Prescriptions 61/2007.
112. Kanta: How can I have a say in the use of my data, How can I have a say in the use of my data?–Citizens–Kanta.fi, 25 Sep. 2022.

279. The same secrecy provisions of patient records are applied to occupational healthcare than to normal healthcare services. However, some exceptions are included in section 18 of Occupational Healthcare Act. Occupational healthcare physician can regardless of what is regulated of secrecy of patient records in Patient's Rights Act give out information to the employer in the case of work with a special risk of illness for the employer. They can also give statements to the occupational safety and health authority and the expert referred to in section 12 of the Act on Occupational Safety and Health Enforcement and Cooperation on Occupational Safety and Health at Workplaces (44/2006) for the purposes of monitoring occupational safety and health. Finally, they can give information to the occupational healthcare service provider for the purposes of monitoring health risks of an employee who has been a patient and been engaged in work causing a special risk of illness.

280. In Finland, employer's right to handle sensitive personal information has been restricted with the Act on Protection of Privacy in Working Life (759/2004). Chapter 2 of the Act includes the common conditions to handle personal information. Section 5 of the Act includes a special provision about handling information about employee's healthcare. The section stipulates that employer has right to handle information about the healthcare of the employee if the information has been gathered from the employee himself/herself or with his/her written consent from somewhere else. These are formal conditions to process healthcare information. In addition, there must be a special reason to handle healthcare information. Section 5 stipulates that the existence of a special reason requires that the information needs to be processed in order to pay sick pay or other comparable health-related benefits or to establish whether there is a justifiable reason for absence or that the employee expressly wishes his/her working capacity to be assessed on the basis of information concerning his/her state of health.

281. The abovementioned are material conditions to handle healthcare information. At least one of the material conditions must be met in order to employer process healthcare information. The employer has also right to process healthcare information in situations and in the width the legislation allows.

282. Employer must be careful when processing healthcare information. This requirement is more strictly regulated in paragraph 2 of section 5 of the Act on Protection of Privacy in Working Life, which stipulates that the employer must nominate persons and specify the tasks which include processing of healthcare information. How the information shall be processed must be agreed in the co-operation bodies of the workplace.

283. The follow-up of absences taken due to illnesses is a responsibility of the employer. Section 10a of the Act on Occupational Healthcare stipulates that employer must inform occupational healthcare services of the employee's absence due to illness not later than after the absence has continued for a month. A statement by occupational healthcare services must be made after employer has informed them about the employee's absence. If employee is a patient to occupational healthcare services and a physician of occupational healthcare services writes a doctor's certificate, employer doesn't have to make a separate notification about employee's absence due to illness.

284. Employee has in certain exceptional cases, a right to receive secret healthcare information about an employee without the consent of the employee. This information can be handled only if it is necessary in order to pay sick pay or other comparable health-related benefit or to establish whether there is a justifiable reason for absence. When an employee himself/herself provides a medical certificate to employer, it indicates the consent that law requires to process information included in the certificate. If the medical certificate is delivered to the employer by a third party, the processing of information requires a precise and written permission of the employee. Even if the employee gives permission to process information about his illness, the processing must be necessary as stipulated in section 3 of the Act on Protection of Privacy in Working Life in order it to be legitimate.

285. It is important for the employee's privacy that the information he/she has delivered to the employer will not be spread. Thus, the employer must keep the healthcare information of employee separate from other personal information he/she has gathered of the employee. Those who handle employee's healthcare information for employer are bound to secrecy about what they have learned and thus cannot express information to a third part during the employment or after it has ended.[113] The representatives of the employee can thus deliver a medical certificate to occupational healthcare services about the employee's ability to provider unless employee has clearly forbidden to hand it out.

§4. Secrecy

286. Section 13 of the Patient's Rights Act (785/1992) imposes secrecy obligation on patient records to any person working in a healthcare unit. Section 13 states that the information contained in patient journals shall be confidential. Healthcare professionals or other persons working in the healthcare unit or carrying out tasks for it, are not allowed to give information contained in patient journals to outsiders without a written consent by the patient. An outsider means a person other than those who participate in the care of the patient or are carrying out jobs related to it in the healthcare unit in question. The secrecy obligation remains in force even after termination of the employment relationship or the job. However, the information included in patient journals may be disclosed, if there are express provisions for it in the legislation. Furthermore, the information necessary for the treatment of the patient may be given to another healthcare unit or healthcare professional. The summary of the provided treatment can be given to the healthcare professional/ healthcare unit that initially referred the patient for treatment and to the physician/

113. Lehtonen L: Terveydentilaa koskevien henkilötietojen käsittely. In Alapuranen L et al. Henkilötietojen käsittely työelämässä, pp. 241–300, Edita 2020.

healthcare unit that will be responsible for the continued care of the patient. For these purposes the consent for disclosure can also be presumed, meaning that the patient has to separately state that those parties shall not receive the information on the treatment that has taken place.

287. A family member or another person close to the patient also may receive information about the state of health of the patient, when the patient is receiving treatment because of unconsciousness or for other comparable reason, unless there is reason to believe that the patient would forbid the disclosure. Furthermore, information on the health and medical care of a deceased person may be disclosed upon a justified written application to anyone who needs the information in order to defend his/her vital interests or rights, to the extent the information is necessary for that purpose. However, the party receiving the information may not use it for any other purposes.

288. However, the Patient's Rights Act is not the only Act containing secrecy requirements for health information. Also, section 17 of the Act on Healthcare Professionals (559/1994) states that a healthcare professional may not without permission disclose to outsiders any secrets of an individual or family that he has learned in his position and tasks. Thus, the requirement for confidentiality is not only restricted to the information in patient journals, but includes any secrets. The secret is defined in the practice in a subjective way meaning anything that the patient wants to keep outside the public sphere. The obligation to maintain confidentiality is a life-long responsibility for a healthcare professional.

289. Also, the Act on the Openness of Government Activities (621/1999) has some important regulations concerning patient journals. This Act is applied for public bodies meaning that also public health centres and hospitals are included. There is a basic provision of secrecy of patient records in section 24 of the act (point 25). However, since the Finnish Constitution guarantees the openness of public administration, also patient records in health centres and hospitals may be asked for public scrutiny. Section 11 of the Act on Openness of Government Activities gives a petitioner's rights even to secret documents, if the document may influence or may have influenced the consideration of his or her matter. However, the documents are not disclosed, if the disclosure is against some other very important private interest. The confidentiality of medical information is considered to be a very important private interest. However, since a petitioner can make a complaint on non-disclosure decisions to an administrative court, the court will finally consider in each case whether the interest for disclosure is greater than the interest for secrecy. E.g., in childcare disputes the Finnish courts have sometimes decided that the interest to look after the benefit of the child is greater than the parent's interest for medical confidentiality.[114]

---

114. THL: Lastensuojelun käsikirja, Uusinta oikeuskäytäntöä, Uusinta oikeuskäytäntöä – THL, 16 Oct. 2022.

§5. COMPLAINTS

290. The Patient's Rights Act also provides legal remedies for the patient. Under section 10, a patient, who is not satisfied with the medical care given to him/her has the right to submit an objection to the director responsible for healthcare in the healthcare unit in question. A decision on claims in the objection must be given in a reasonable time. Submitting an objection to a healthcare unit does not restrict the patient's right to appeal later to the supervising authorities.

291. Section 10a of the Patient's Rights Act includes the right for the patient to complain to the Regional State Administrative Agency or to the National Supervisory Authority for Welfare and Health (Valvira), if the patient still feels unsatisfied after receiving a response to the objection. In the cases, where no prior objection has been made, the supervising authorities may, however, transfer the complaint to the healthcare unit in question to be handled first as an objection.

292. Currently, section 11 of the Patient's Rights Act requires that a patient ombudsman shall be appointed for each healthcare unit.[115] His tasks include also advising and helping the patients in cases of objections and complaints.

115. HUS: Patient ombudsmen, https://www.hus.fi/en/patient/patient-guide/your-rights-patient/patient-ombudsmen, 26 Oct. 2022.

Chapter 2. The Physician: Patient Relationship in Specific Terms

§1. The Minor Patient

293. According to section 7 of the Patient's Rights Act, the opinion of a minor patient on a treatment measure has to be assessed if it is possible with regard to his/her age or level of development. If a minor patient owing to his/her age and level of development can decide on the treatment given to him/her, he/she has to be cared in mutual understanding with him/her. However, if a minor patient cannot decide on the treatment given to him/her, he/she has to be cared in mutual understanding with his/her guardian or legal representative. Also, section 4 of the Act of Child Custody and Right of Access (361/1983) states that parents or legal guardians of the child have the responsibility on the medical treatment for the child.

294. A minor may be capable of making decisions on his/her treatment without the consent of the parents. Minor patient's ability to influence on decisions concerning themselves may be divided into three categories: (1) self-determination, in which the patient's consent is enough for legal capability, (2) parents' consent is needed, (3) minor's opinion must be heard, and the opinion taken into consideration in accordance with age and level of development.[116]

295. The minor patient in Finland has the right to self-determination, when a physician finds him/her capable of understanding the treatment and its effects.[117] When this is the case, the patient must be treated in agreement with him/her and not just according to the will of the parents. The patient's age, as well as their level of development, effects on the decision whether or not the minor patient is capable of exercising the right to self-determination, and the nature of the procedure must as well be taken into consideration.[118] In practice, a twelve-year-old is usually considered mature enough to have the right to self-determination. However, the opinion of a children under 12 years of age must be taken into consideration when he/she challenges the treatment decisions.[119] Another possible age limit for exercising the right to self-determination has been found to be 15 years old, which is the age limit for independent consent in the Act on Medical Research. However, there is no fixed age limit when a minor is capable of exercising the right to self-determination in medical treatment. This is shown in the decision given by the Parliamentary Ombudsman in 2015, where he emphasized that there is no set age in legislation when evaluating minor's capability for exercising the right to self-determination, but the crucial element in the assessment is whether the patient is able to understand the effects of the treatment and declining from it. The patient's maturity is one of the

116. Aaltonen A–K: Lapsioikeus ja lapsen oikeus tuomioistuimessa, pp. 241–242, Helsinki 2009.
117. Nordic Legal Research Group on Health Law: Patient's consent to treatment – a nordic perspective on medical self-determination, Report from Finland, Nordic_LRG_Medical_Law.pdf (elsa.org), 16 Oct. 2022.
118. Government proposal, 185/1991 vp. p. 18.
119. Hannuniemi A: Alaikäisen oikeudellisesta asemasta terveydenhuollossa, Lakimies 6/1997, p. 842.

criteria amongst their level of development, and the possible risks of the operation.[120] In the literature, the criteria for a minor being capable for exercising the right to self-determination are described as following; they are mature enough to consider the treatment, they have had enough information on different treatments and their effects, they have considered the issue with care, and the minor has stated their will and opinion without any pressure or coercion.[121] Thus the evaluation of a child's competence to make decisions on medical treatment should always be based on the overall assessment of the child's maturity. When consenting to treatment the minor must have appropriate knowledge on treatment options and the possible effects of those, the minor has considered with care, and expressed their will without any outside coercion or pressure.[122]

296. The child's full right to self-determination would mean that they have the right to decide matters concerning them in contradiction to their benefit. A minor's will, when competent for self-determination, may not be side-lined because the parents have a different view on how the treatment should be conducted.[123] On the other hand, childcare authorities have to power to protect the child's health even in the cases where he/she is not consenting to the treatment. If a legal guardian or parents of the minor refuse on a treatment, which according to medical professionals would be necessary for the health and life of the patient, the child may be taken into custody and the consent to the treatment would be given by childcare authorities. In a judgment given by the Supreme Administrative Court of Finland in 1991, in which the minor had leukaemia and was in need for immediate blood transfer, which the minor's both parents objected, the court adjudicated that the child could be taken into custody and be hospitalized so the treatment could be accomplished.[124] In another similar judgment, the Supreme Administrative Court adjudicated that a child suffering from lymphoma could be taken into custody since the minor's parents refused on giving blood products for the child, and the Court stated that it was necessary on preventing danger on the child's life or health.[125]

297. When a minor is incapable of deciding on their own medical treatment, he/she should be treated in agreement with the parents or the legal guardian. When the child has two parents, both of them must make the decision together.[126] In the Administrative Court judgment given in 2003, the Court ruled that both parents' approval for therapy was necessary, and that when the parents are disagreeing on

---

120. Parliamentary Ombudsman EOA 11 Jun. 2015 Dnro 61/4/15.
121. Helin M: Alaikäisen oikeudet potilaana. In Koivisto J, Potilaan oikeudet ja potilasasiamiestoiminta, p. 92, Suomen Kuntaliiton julkaisu 1994.
122. Kirsi Pollari K and Lohiniva-Kerkelä M: Ketä kuullaan–Kuka päättää? Alaikäisen osallisuus ja itsemääräämisoikeus terveyden- ja sairaanhoidossa. In Suvianna Hakalehto-Wainio S and Nieminen L, Lapsioikeus murroksessa, p. 287. Lakimiesliiton kustannus 2013.
123. Nordic Legal Research Group on Health Law: Patient's consent to treatment–a nordic perspective on medical self-determination, Nordic_LRG_Medical_Law.pdf (elsa.org), 16 Oct. 2022.
124. Supreme Administrative Court KHO 9 Aug. 1991 T 2542.
125. Supreme Administrative Court KHO 10 Mar. 2000/530 Dnro 2385/99.
126. Section 5, Act on Child Custody and Right of Access (361/1983).

the treatment, the treatment cannot be given just as an agreement between one parent and the doctor.[127] However, before the parent makes the decision on medical treatment given to the minor, the child must be heard and their opinion and wishes has to be taken into consideration.[128] According to the legal framework, it is mandatory to take into consideration the child's opinion due to principle according to which parents must gradually give more and more independency and so secure the child's growth towards their adulthood.[129]

298. In a decision given by the Deputy Parliamentary Ombudsman, she stated that treatment given to a seven-year-old who was in foster care, should have been done in consensus with the biological parents, and child welfare services. When the doctor, who had treated the child and prescribed medication to him, had argued that the parents of the child should not be informed on the treatment, the Deputy Parliamentary Ombudsman found it to be illegal, since a minor who is not capable of exercising the right to self-determination must be treated in agreement with their parents.[130]

299. The Child Welfare Act (417/2007) makes it mandatory for healthcare professional to report to child protection authorities any child whose development is endangered by circumstances or by the child's behaviour. This could also include cases where the child is not adequately treated for a medical problem. According to section 40 of the Child Welfare Act, a child must be taken into care and substitute care must be provided for them by the municipal body responsible for social services if his/her health or development is seriously endangered by lack of care or other circumstances in which they are being brought up. If the child is taken into care by child protection authorities, they also have the power (Child Welfare Act, section 45) to decide on the necessary healthcare for the child.[131]

§2. The Mental Patients

300. The Mental Health Act (1116/1990) that was enforced in 1991 aims to improve outpatient care and decrease long hospitalizations of mental patients. Section 5 of the Act (as changed in the Mental Health Act by the Act 1066/2009) emphasizes the co-operation of different parties in health and social care. In addition to sufficient psychiatric treatment, the patients should have possibility to medicinal and social rehabilitation and service housing.

301. Some patients, who are extremely hard to handle (especially forensic psychiatric patients, who are not convicted on a crime due to non-compos mentis), are

127. HAO 8 Nov. 2003 T 93/0837/2.
128. Act on Child Custody and Right of Access, §4.2.
129. Government proposal, 224/1982 vp. p. 14.
130. Parliamentary Ombudsman EOA 4.9.2020 Dnro 7210/2019.
131. Nordic Legal Research Group on Health Law: Patient's consent to treatment–a nordic perspective on medical self–determination, Report from Finland, Nordic_LRG_Medical_Law.pdf (elsa.org), 16 Oct. 2022.

treated in state mental hospitals. Two state mental hospitals are still maintained: The mental hospital of Vanha Vaasa and the mental hospital of Niuvaniemi (Act on State Mental Hospitals 1292/1987). The National Institute for Health and Welfare makes a decision to take a forensic psychiatric patient into state mental hospital. Other hard-to-handle patients may be taken into state mental hospitals. if the hospital district so proposes.

302. Section 1 of the Mental Health Act defines mental health work as the promotion of the mental wellbeing, ability to cope and personal growth of the individual, and the prevention, curing and alleviation of mental illnesses and other mental disorders. Mental healthcare services must primarily be organized as outpatient services. Mental healthcare services must also be organized in such a manner that the willingness to seek treatment comes from patient him/herself and that the treatment supports independent management.

303. The Mental Health Act emphasizes the legal protection of psychiatric patients taken into treatment against their will. Section 8 of the Mental Health Act stipulates that a person can be ordered in a psychiatric hospital against his or her will only if the person is diagnosed mentally ill and if the person needs treatment for a mental illness which, if not treated, would become considerably worse or severely endanger the person's health or safety or the health or safety of others. Furthermore, the third prerequisite for compulsory treatment demands that all other mental health services are inapplicable or inadequate for the patients.

304. Mental illness in section 8 of the Act can be defined as a serious disturbance of the mind, which includes clear disturbance of sense of realism. The international classification of diseases considers different forms of schizophrenia, organic and other states of delusion, severe depression, bipolar disorder, states of delirium, advanced states of dementia and other psychiatric diseases as mental illnesses.

305. In order to send a patient to involuntary psychiatric treatment, physician must write a specific referral (sc. M1 form) for compulsory treatment. In it the physician must demonstrate that the requirements of involuntary psychiatric treatment are fulfilled. A physician working in public health centre has a duty based on his/her official post as stipulated in the section 29 of Mental Health Act to issue a referral in these cases. The police are obliged to give executive assistance to transport the patient to a health centre, although the transport should mainly be done by an ambulance and with assistance of healthcare professionals.[132]

132. Supreme Administrative Court, record number KHO 2012:63: A purchase service doctor who had issued the referral for observation for A, did not have the competence to send A to treatment against his/her will be in order to discover whether the conditions to order A to hospital treatment were met, because the purchase service didn't hold an office at the municipality and the competence of a purchase service doctor wasn't stated in the legislation. Since the decision to take A into observation wasn't based on a referral issued by a physician holding an office, the decision to order A into treatment wasn't made according to the Constitution and Mental Health Act.

306. Based on the M1 referral (i.e., not older than three days) a physician can take the patient into observation in a psychiatric hospital. At latest, on the fourth day after taking the patient into observation, a psychiatrist must issue a written statement (M2-statement), which must include a reasonable description whether the criteria of involuntary treatment are met. If it is found during the observation, that the criteria are not met, the patient must be discharged from the hospital if he/she so wishes.[133]

307. The physician in charge of the psychiatric treatment in the hospital makes the decision about the compulsory treatment (the M3-statement) based on the observation report. The opinion of the patient or, in case the patient is a minor, the guardian of the patient must be heard before the decision on the compulsory treatment is made. The physician who issued the referral to observation cannot give the observation report, and the physician, who made the observation report, cannot make the administrative decision on compulsory treatment. Thus, according to the Mental Health Act, the decision on compulsory psychiatric treatment is always based on three different physician's view about the necessity of the treatment. In addition, in the case 3.7.2012 *X v. Finland,* the European Human Rights Court has stated that the patient must have a possibility to have an estimation made by an independent physician outside the hospital circles when assessing the need for compulsory treatment in an administrative court.[134]

308. Before making the decision about the compulsory treatment, the patient must be heard if it is medically possible, and the patient can understand the meaning of the decision. Compulsory treatment is usually not possible, if the patient agrees voluntarily to stay in the psychiatric treatment.

309. Also, a minor person under 18 years of age can be ordered into involuntary treatment, if he/she has a mental disorder or other serious mental disturbance. If the child is so young that he/she cannot make decisions on his/her treatment, the guardians can make the appropriate decision. However, a person under 18-years-old can be ordered into psychiatric treatment also without the consent of the guardians. They must, however, be heard either orally or in writing before the decision on compulsory treatment.

---

133. Supreme Administrative Court, record number KHO 2006:85: The observation to discover whether the conditions to order the patient into treatment against his/her will are met could only be executed in a hospital. The psychiatric treatment ordered to patient against his/her will could only be executed in a hospital unit providing psychiatric treatment. The observation had been executed so that the patient, who wasn't removed from the hospital records, had not been in a hospital. After leaving the hospital, his/her treatment had been restricted to scheduled visits at the hospital in order to receive medication via injections. His/her residency outside the hospital wasn't a so called 'experimental treatment-holiday' but a permanent residency. The observation wasn't executed and the treatment ordered against his/her will wasn't organized according to the Act. The treatment to which the patient was ordered against his/her will had ended on the day the patient had left the hospital.
134. ECHR: Case of *X v. Finland*, http://hudoc.echr.coe.int/sites/eng/pages/search.aspx?i=001-111938, 4 Oct. 2022.

310. The physician-in-chief in the hospital can make a decision to take a mentally ill patient to compulsory psychiatric treatment for maximum three months. The compulsory treatment can be extended with a new decision that must be based on a new observation report and made before the previous treatment period has ended. The extension of the treatment can be maximum six months long. The decision to continue compulsory treatment must however be submitted to administrative court for enforcement. If the criteria for compulsory treatment are no longer met, the treatment must immediately be ended and the patient discharged from the hospital if he/she so wishes. In legal praxis, the formal conditions to continue treatment are interpreted tightly.[135]

311. The Finnish Constitution requires that any restrictions of the basic rights must be based on parliamentary legislation. Therefore, the Mental Health Act has precise regulations concerning any involuntary measures that can be performed during the compulsory treatment in a psychiatric hospital. Involuntary measures can be taken already during the observatory period, if they are necessary to protect the health of the patient. All possible restrictions and intrusions are listed in Chapter 4a of Mental Health Act. In this chapter (1423/2001), the self-determination rights of a patient in compulsory treatment have been updated to the standards set by the Constitution and European Convention on Human Rights. Since different emergency acts and their conditions are stipulated in the law, the regulation of coercive treatment has become quite detailed. The restrictive measures must be medically justifiable. The emergency actions can only be used to the limit which the treatment of the patient, his/her or someone else's safety or the protection of other important interest listed in Chapter 4a of the Act necessarily requires. It is crucial to estimate the proportionality of the actions when considering the acceptability of emergency actions. In addition, the restrictive measures must always be done with a respect to patient's dignity.

312. The patient's right for self-determination can be restrictive only for medical reasons or to ensure safety of the patient or other person or for another interest stipulated in the Chapter 4a of the Act. This means that the jurisdiction stipulated in Chapter 4a cannot be used for other purposes than what is clearly stipulated. For example, the use of restrictive measures as punishments is forbidden. The section 22b of Mental Health Act sets two additional requirements to the involuntary treatment: Medically acceptable methods must be used in the treatment of the patient.

135. The Supreme Administrative Court KHO 2011:70: A decision to continue H's treatment as stipulated in s. 17 para. 2 of Mental Health Act was made 2 Jun. 2010, and administrative court hade enforced it with its decision. As stipulated in s. 17 para. 2 of Mental Health Act, the decision to continue or end H's treatment in hospital had to be done by a physician's written decision before the treatment had lasted for six months that is by latest 2 Dec. 2010. The chief physician had made the decision to continue treatment not until 5.1.2011 on the basis of an observation report given the same day, that is after the deadline stipulated in s. 17 para. 2 of Mental Health Act. The physician could not have made the decision about H's treatment on 5 Jan. 2011 in the order stipulated in the Act. The fact that H had run away from the hospital during the treatment and had been unreachable before the deadline was met wasn't relevant. Thus, the Supreme Administrative Court overruled administrative ruling and left the submitted decision to continue treatment without enforcement.

This refers to the obligation to follow commonly accepted and empirically justified standards as stipulated in the Act on Healthcare Professionals. In addition, the measures must be so crucial that if they are not taken, it will seriously endanger the safety and health of the patient or of other people.

313. The mental state and competence of the patient are the crucial to determine the significance of his/her own wishes. If the patient is capable to decide on his/her own treatment and clearly is against of certain procedures, the section 6 of Patient's Rights Act stipulates that he/she should be treated with such a medically acceptable method which he/she approves. However, usually patients, who have been ordered to compulsory psychiatric treatment, are not capable to make decisions on their treatment. The Mental Health Act does not set an obligation to hear patient's family or legal representatives or to acquire consent from them for the treatment. However, co-operation with the family is an integral part of good quality care, even though confidentiality requirements on the health status of the patient apply also against the family members.

314. During the observation period and compulsory treatment, the patient must have opportunities to exercise outdoors and exercise physically. Section 22 of the Mental Health Act stipulates that a patient can be restrained from leaving the hospital area or the spaces of a certain unit. If patient leaves the hospital area without permission or does not return at the agreed time, he/she can be brought back. To prevent patient from leaving hospital, the staff of the healthcare unit can use such necessary force that can be considered defendable. Furthermore, section 31 of the Mental Health Act stipulates that the police must give assistance to bring the runaway patient back to hospital. In the healthcare unit, the decision to restrain patient's liberty to leave from or move within the hospital area is made by the physician in charge of the patient.

315. Section 22e of the Mental Health Act permits the usage of special restrictive measures to a patient in compulsory psychiatric treatment. These restrictions are adherence and isolation from other patients. In exceptional cases, a patient can also be bound that is set to strait jacket. To calm an agitated patient down with medication is not separately mentioned as a special restriction since it is difficult to separate medicinal treatment for appeasement from other involuntary medical treatment stipulated in section 22b of the Mental Health Act. The ECHR has found the Finnish practice of using compulsory medications during the observation period unjustified which should be revised by including a specific regulation on medication into the Mental Health Act.[136]

316. Isolation means that a patient is shut away either in his/her own room or in another locked room. The usage of isolation is allowed if the patient's actions or made threats suggest that he/she probably would harm either him/herself or other

136. Valtioneuvosto: EIT:n tuomio tahdosta riippumatonta hoitoa ja pakkolääkitystä koskevassa asiassa, https://valtioneuvosto.fi/-/eit-n-tuomio-tahdosta-riippumatonta-hoitoa-ja-pakkolaakitysta-koskevassa-asiassa, 26 Oct. 2022.

people. This means patient's self-destructive or violent behaviour. The evaluation of the situation is based on the competence or experience of the staff. Isolation is also allowed, if the patient's behaviour makes it much more difficult to treat other patients or endangers his/her own safety. Such behaviour could be for example the harassment of other patients. A damage made to property is usually considered as an aggravation of other patients' treatment. Patient can also be isolated if it is necessary for other cogent reason related to treatment, for example, if common stimulus or social situations worsen the illness of the patient. However, the proper environment should be organized for the patients.

317. A patient in compulsory treatment can be bound with a belt or put to strait-jacket, if the patient otherwise would probably harm him/herself or other people. This is, however, allowed only in extreme cases.

318. The decision on the isolation and binding of the patient is made by a physician. When action must be taken to settle imminent danger and the physician is not available, a member of the staff can isolate or bind the patient temporarily. The physician must, however, be immediately informed then decide whether to continue the procedure after examining the patient. These procedures cannot be approved beforehand.

319. The restrictive measure must be stopped immediately after it is not deemed to be necessary. The physician who is in charge of the patient must regularly examine the state of isolated or bound patient and decide whether to continue or discontinue the restriction. The state of the isolated patient must be evaluated at least twice a day and a bound patient's state must be evaluated even more often. The Parliamentary Ombudsman is inspecting in his visits, whether the restrictions have been performed appropriately.[137]

320. Drugs or tools that are suitable for drug use or substances or other items that might endanger the safety or health of the patient, other patients or staff can be taken into the possession of the healthcare unit during the compulsory psychiatric treatment. A member of the hospital staff can seize substances and items when she/he founds them. The physician in charge must immediately be informed, and the physician must decide whether the property can be returned to the patient before the treatment ends or not. Information about what the property was and why it was seized must be clearly documented in patient records. Seizure of property in the hospital is so-called practical administrative action without a possibility to appeal to courts. The seized property must be returned after the treatment has ended, unless it is otherwise regulated in the legislation.

137. *See* Parliamentary Ombudsman 1 Nov. 2012, record number 4102/4/11: The reason why instead of isolation patient had been bound wasn't clearly enough stated on the patient records. Unnecessary deprivation of liberty had also taken place when the patient wasn't allowed to do outdoor exercise for five weeks.

321. If there are reasonable grounds to suspect that the patient has drugs or forbidden items in his/her possession, the rooms and property he/she has in his/her possession can be searched. In addition, a letter or other delivery addressed to the patient can be checked if there are reasonable grounds to suspect that the letter or delivery contains drugs or other forbidden items. The physician in charge of the patient's treatment makes the decision to perform the search.

322. A search or inspection targeted to a person is coercive measure to find out what the inspected has in his/her clothes or otherwise on him/her. A patient who has been taken into observation or to compulsory treatment may be searched if it is suspected that he/she is wearing substances or items that may endanger safety or treatment. According to the Coercive Measures Act (806/2011), a search of a person consists of a body search, taking a blood sample and other examination targeted to the body. A search may be targeted to a patient in compulsory psychiatric care, if there are reasonable grounds to suspect that the patient has used substances or that he/she has them or other forbidden items hidden in his/her body. Taking a sample or performing a test may not cause unnecessary harm for the patient. The decision to perform a search on a person is made by the physician in charge of the patient. The search must be done in the presence of two healthcare professionals who are members of the staff. A search targeted to a person can be performed only by a healthcare professional and an examination that requires medical expertise only by a physician.

323. In general, a psychiatric patient has the right to keep contact with people outside the hospital. This right is linked with the protection of patient's private life, family life and confidential message, which are secured both in the Finnish Constitution and in international human rights conventions. The restrictions to communication must be based on a parliamentary act and their interpretation is strict. However, the provision doesn't prevent the healthcare service provider to set restrictions for visits and for phone usage in order to organize the treatment (e.g., that phone use only in certain spaces is allowed). Communication may be restricted, if it causes serious damage for the patient's treatment, rehabilitation, or safety or it is necessary to protect another person's private life. However, the communication to supervisory authorities cannot be restricted. Furthermore, the communication between patient and his/her legal representative and or hospital's patient ombudsman cannot be restricted at all. The equipment and tools used for communicative purposes that are in the patient's possession can be seized or their usage may be restricted during the compulsory treatment. These tools and equipment include mobile phones and computers.

324. The chief physician or other physician in similar position in the hospital makes the decision to restrict patient's communication. Before making the decision, the patient must be given a chance to say his/her opinion about the matter. Also, the other party of the communication, if known to the hospital, must be given a chance to say his/her opinion. The decision must clearly state the reasons for the restriction and the parties to whom the restriction is used and the width of the measure. The decision of the restriction is made only for a defined time, which can be maximally 30 days at a time.

325. When a patient has been taken into compulsory psychiatric treatment and is not competent to make decisions concerning his/her somatic treatment, the consent for the somatic treatment must be asked from his/her representative or next of kin or from another close person as stipulated in section 6 paragraphs 2 and 3 of the Patient's Rights Act. In the cases of urgent treatment, however, the consent of patient's representative isn't required. Even then the opinion the patient has previously expressed must be considered. The physician in charge makes the decisions of somatic treatment. If the treatment is given in another healthcare unit than in psychiatric hospital, the physician in charge of the treatment in that unit makes the decisions about the treatment and the procedures required. In another unit than in psychiatric hospital, the physician making the decisions must work in co-operation with the physician who is in charge of the psychiatric treatment of the patient.

326. The Mental Health Act includes four administrative actions that one can appeal of. These are: the order to compulsory treatment, the continuation of compulsory treatment, the seizure of property and the restriction of communication. The patient may appeal of these decisions to the administrative court. The quorum of the court in these matters must include an expert member (psychiatrist) as stipulated in section 7 of the Administrative Courts Act (430/1997). The appeal to administrative court must be made in two weeks after the abovementioned decision. The letter of appeal which can be informal must include the name and contact address of the appellant (or of the supervisory of the interest), the decision which is appealed of and the grounds for the appeal. To draft the letter of appeal, the patient can get assistance from the patient ombudsman. The appeal should be left for the administrative court but can also be delivered for the chief in charge of psychiatry to be forwarded to the court.

327. The decisions about binding and isolation are not appealable. These operations aim to control immediately dangerous situations and they are considered practical administrative actions. Instead of appealing, the patient can make a reprimand stipulated in the Patient's Rights Act or an administrative complaint. In addition to binding and isolation, personal search is also a practical administrative action of which patient cannot appeal, but the available legal protection is either a reprimand stipulated in the Patient's Rights Act, or a complaint addressed to the supervisory authority.

328. To make the supervision of the restrictions feasible, the psychiatric hospital must keep a list of the restrictions in the healthcare unit where the patient is treated. The list must include the identification information of the patient, information about the restrictions and the names of the physician who permitted the measures and of those who performed the required measures. In addition, the information on the isolation and binding of patients must be sent every two weeks to the Regional State Administrative Agency. The notification to the Agency must include the identification information of the patient in question, information on the performed measures and the grounds for them and the name of the physician who permitted the measures.

§3. The Dying Patient

329. There are no specific regulations concerning dying patients in Finland. The Patient's Rights Act guarantees for the competent adult patient the right to refuse treatment even when the refusal will lead to the death of the patient. The patient's right to self-determination means that he or she can refuse any treatment that has already been planned or started. The right to discontinue treatment also applies to situations which result in the patient's death, serious injury, serious illness, or risk of such illness.[138] It is a key part of self-determination that a person is allowed to live and die by the individual's perceptions, beliefs and values. If the patient refuses a life-saving treatment, he or she must be cared for, as far as possible, in another medically acceptable way in mutual understanding with him or her (Patient's Rights Act, section 6).

330. According to section 3 of the Patient's Rights Act, every patient has the right to good medical treatment which extends to end-of-life care as well. When a patient is close to dying, one of the most important aims of treatment is to alleviate pain and suffering. Often it is medically sensible to stop treatment since emergency medical care can be highly invasive on the body. If the patient is not conscious, their relatives or people close must be notified of the situation. A Do-Not-Resuscitate (DNR) decision is an important treatment decision that is always made individually for each patient. The decision is based on a medical assessment of the patient's condition and prognosis that are based on the physician's education and experience. The patient's age or diagnosis are not critical in the decision. The DNR decision should be made jointly by a doctor and a patient. The DNR decision can also be discussed with the patient's relative or another close person with the patient's consent. In principle, however, the patient's relative or other close person is an outsider. If a patient is unable to contribute to the decisions concerning the care, the consent of patient's legal representative, a close relative or another close person should be asked as provided in section 6 of the Patient's Rights Act. The decision to discontinue the active treatment is ultimately at the discretion of the physician, since he is always obliged to follow the medical standards. When the physician considers that it is not in the patient's interest to continue the treatment, active treatments are stopped, even if the person in the position of deputy decision-maker would demand further treatment. The consensus requirement on the treatment is based on the best interests of the patient.[139] With the advance directive, a patient may continue to use their self-determination even when they are not competent anymore. Infirmity and high age are not factors which would remove the competent to decide on their own treatment

---

138. Pahlman I: Potilaan itsemääräämisoikeus, pp. 214–215, Edita Publishing Oy 2003.
139. Pahlman, Irma: Itsemääräämisoikeus, In: Lehtonen L et al., Terveysoikeus, Alma Talent 2015, pp. 206–207.

in end-of-life care. When treating older patients, the doctor should make sure that he is following the patient's wishes, and not the opinions of the family member, who is acting as a proxy, since legal representative or other close person for the patient are required to follow the will of the patient in their instructions.[140]

331. Thus, the treating physician is ultimately responsible for the medical decisions concerning the treatment in Finland. Even if the healthcare proxy demands on continuing the treatment, the physician may decide to end the treatment when those are not anymore benefitting the patient. However, active euthanasia is not allowed in Finland even though the issue has been discussed in the parliament based on a citizen initiative.[141]

140. Nordic Legal Research Group on Health Law: Patient's consent to treatment–a nordic perspective on medical self-determination, Report from Finland, Nordic_LRG_Medical_Law.pdf (elsa.org), 16 Oct. 2022.

141. Eduskunta: Eduskunta hylkäsi kansalaisaloitteen ehdotuksen eutanasian sallimisesta, Eduskunta hylkäsi kansalaisaloitteen ehdotuksen eutanasian sallimisesta, 11 Oct. 2022.

Chapter 3. Specific Activities

§1. Abortion

332. Finland belongs to countries with liberal practices concerning abortion. This development started already in early 70s when the Act on the Termination of Pregnancy (the Abortion Act, 239/1970) was approved. Section 1 of the Act lists several reasons for the termination of pregnancy based on the request of the pregnant woman. These include the disease or poor health of the mother, if the pregnancy endangers her life of health. The so-called social reason for abortion stipulates that the birth and care of the child would cause considerable stress for her when considering the living conditions in the family and other circumstances. Furthermore, the pregnancy can be terminated, if the pregnancy is a result of rape, sexual abuse or child abuse. Pregnancy can also be terminated on the request of the pregnant woman, if her age is under 17 years when the pregnancy has started or at least 40 years or if she already has given birth to at least four children. The pregnancy can also be terminated, if it is reason to believe that the child would have a mental defect, severe disease, or malformation. Finally, the pregnancy can be terminated, if the disease of each or both parents, their mental capacity or other corresponding reason would severely limit their ability to care the child.

333. In medical practice In Finland, the social reason has been interpreted in a way that the wish for abortion by the pregnant woman is an adequate reason for the termination of the pregnancy. The physicians are not required to do any kind of background check, but since at least two doctors are involved in the decision to terminate a pregnancy, the wish of the pregnant woman for abortion will be verified on several occasions. However, the requirement of the opinion of two doctors is due to change in abortions up to week twelve of the pregnancy.[142] Section 4 of the Act stipulates that before the pregnancy is terminated, the pregnant woman should receive information on meaning and effects of the abortion.[143]

334. Section 5 of the Abortion Act stipulates that if pregnancy will be terminated, it should be done as early in the pregnancy as possible. Termination of pregnancy is not allowed after twelve weeks of pregnancy, unless it is necessary to protect the life and health of the pregnant woman. If the pregnancy is causing imminent danger for the life and health of the pregnant woman, the abortion can be carried out without any time limit. Furthermore, the National Supervisory Authority for Welfare and Health can authorize abortion up to twenty-four weeks of pregnancy, if it is verified with amniocentesis or ultrasound or other reliable examinations that the foetus has a severe developmental disorder. In other cases, the abortion is usually carried out based on the decision of two physicians. Section 6 of the Abortion Act states that one of the deciding physicians is any physician working in public health

142. Eduskunta: Sosiaali- ja terveysvaliokunta ehdottaa muutoksia aborttilakiin OmaTahto2020 -kansalaisaloitteen pohjalta, Sosiaali- ja terveysvaliokunta ehdottaa muutoksia aborttilakiin OmaTahto2020 -kansalaisaloitteen pohjalta (eduskunta.fi), 11 Oct. 2022.
143. Burrell, Riitta: Naisia ja sikiöitä. Helsinki 2003.

centres or hospitals or a physician (usually a gynaecologist) that has got the permission from the National Supervisory Authority for Welfare and Health to make decisions concerning abortions. He/she is the one that refers the woman to a hospital gynaecologist. The other physician making decisions on abortions is the physician (gynaecologist) that is carrying out the abortion in hospital. However, in the cases where the abortion is based on young or old age of the pregnant woman or on the number of previous children (at least four), the decision of the physician carrying out the abortion is adequate. Furthermore, in the cases where the abortion is carried out after rape or child abuse, the authorization for abortion is given by the National Authority of Health and Welfare.

335. In rare cases, an abortion can be authorized also by the guardian of the pregnant woman. Section 2 of the Abortion Act states that if the pregnant woman lacks the competence due to psychiatric disease or mental defect, also the guardian of the woman can apply for abortion. The father of the child has little to say to termination of pregnancy in Finland. Section 7 of the Abortion Act states that the father may be given a possibility to tell his opinion, if there is reason for a hearing. However, in practice the decision on abortion is based on the opinion of the pregnant woman also when considering the social reasons for the abortion, like family conditions.

336. Even though the practice for abortion is liberal in Finland and pregnant women have no difficulties to find a hospital for them, the administrative process of demanding two physicians to make decisions is considered obsolete. This praxis is now due to change and abortions for social reasons will be possible with the decision of one doctor will be possible up to twelve weeks of pregnancy from 1 January 2023.[144] Most abortions are nowadays carried out using abortion pills reducing the medical risks that were associated with surgical abortion. The abortion policies in Finland have been reasonably successful, since the number of abortions especially among young women have been decreasing for years (but also the birth rate has been decreasing). This is a result of sexual education and availability of contraceptive methods. Contraceptive advice is also given after abortion. In 2019 there were some 8,700 abortions in Finland.[145] Of these, over one-third is, however, performed to women that have had at least one previous abortion.

337. In Finland, the number of abortions is followed by the National Supervisory Authority for Welfare and Health that keeps a national registry on abortions.[146] This registry is based on the Act of National Supervisory Authority for Welfare and Health (668/2008) and on the functions of the Authority in the field of health statistics

---

144. Sosiaali- ja terveysvaliokunnan mietintö StVM 16/2022 vp – KAA 8/2020 vp, StVM 16/2022 vp (eduskunta.fi), 18 Dec. 2022.
145. Tiitinen A: Raskaudenkeskeytys, https://www.terveyskirjasto.fi/dlk00166, 11 Oct. 2022.
146. Terveyden ja hyvinvoinnin laitos: Raskaudenkeskeyttämisrekisteri, https://thl.fi/fi/tilastot-ja-data/aineistot-ja-palvelut/rekisterien-tietosuojailmoitukset/raskaudenkeskeytykset, 11.10.2022.

§2. STERILIZATION

338. The Finnish Sterilization Act (28371970) dates toyear 1970. It was accepted at the same time as the Abortion Act. The legislation before had a background in racial hygiene doctrine and was used to sterilize people with handicaps and even with psychiatric problems. Some 7,500 people were sterilized in Finland between 1935 and 1970 even though these practices were abandoned before the legislation was changed.

339. The current Sterilization Act considers sterilization more as a contraceptive method. According to the revised version section 1 of the Act (from 1985), sterilization is possible by request of the person in question, when the person has at least 3 children under 18 years or when he/she is at least 30 years old. Sterilization is also possible if pregnancy would be a risk for the life or health of the person in question. Furthermore, sterilization is possible also, if other contraceptive methods would work unusually poorly for the person.

340. In addition to the contraceptive purposes, the Sterilization Act lists other reasons for sterilization. Sterilization is possible, if there are good reasons to believe that his/her offspring would have a serious disease of malformation or when his/her disease or other corresponding reason severely restricts his/her ability to take care of children. Finally, sterilization is possible in cases, where the person feels belonging to another gender and lives in that sexual role (transgender person).

341. Sterilization due to reasons mentioned in section 1 of the Act requires that either one or two physicians make the decision on the procedure. When sterilization is carried out based on the age of the person or when the number of children is three of more, the decision of the physician who is performing sterilization is adequate. If sterilization is carried out because pregnancy would be dangerous or when other contraceptive methods are not suitable for the person, the joint decision of two physicians is required. This is the case also when sterilization is performed for a transgender person. In cases where the request for sterilization is based on possible serious disease of malformation of the offspring or due to the inability of the person to take care of possible children, the decision is made by the National Supervisory Authority for Welfare and Health.

342. If the person is permanently unable to understand the meaning of sterilization, also the guardian can ask for sterilization. Sterilization on the request of a guardian is very rare, but can be used for mentally retarded persons with high sexual drive.

343. If the person asking sterilization is married, also the spouse may be heard before the sterilization procedure. Section 3 of the Sterilization Act states that a hearing might be necessary to find out, to whom of the married couple is suggested the sterilization procedure. About two-thirds of the about 4,500 annual sterilizations in Finland are done to male patients, and about one-third to female patients.[147] The men undergoing sterilization tend to be somewhat older (their mean age is around 40 years) than women (mean age around 36 years). Even though surgical sterilization can be dissolved, and the fertility of the patient restored, it is very important to verify before the sterilization procedure that the patient is not aiming to have children.

§3. In Vitro Fertilization

344. The Act on In Vitro Fertilization (1237/2006) was approved in 2006 after a lengthy preparation.[148] The Act was part of implementation of the regulations of the Biomedicine Convention of the Council of Europe into the Finnish legislation. The Act includes the prohibition of human cloning in its section 4. Furthermore, section 4 of the Act also restricts the genetic manipulation of the gametes or embryos that are used in vitro fertilization.

345. The Act defines In Vitro Fertilization (IVF) to be a procedure where gametes or embryos are inserted into female body to induce pregnancy. The service provider that provides in vitro fertilization services must have a specific permission for the activities given by the National Authority of Health and Welfare. The Act regulates the storage of gametes and embryos and their disposal for in vitro fertilization. The basic principle in Finnish legislation is that gametes and embryos are destroyed after the death of the donor.

346. Section 8 of the Act lists the cases, where in vitro fertilization is not allowed in Finland. These include the lack of written consent of the gamete donor. In vitro fertilization is also not possible in cases, where one of the parties participating in vitro fertilization is married or in corresponding relation with a third party. Furthermore, in vitro fertilization is not possible, if pregnancy due to the age or health of the mother would cause considerable danger to the mother or to the child. Even though not stated exactly in the Act, the age limit for women in public healthcare is usually 40 years, but some private clinics take mother candidates up to 46 years in their in vitro fertilization treatment. For male patients, the age limit for IVF therapy in public healthcare is 60 years. If there is reason to believe that the child will not have balanced development or if there is reason to believe that the child will be given for adoption, in vitro fertilization is not allowed. The requirement for balanced development of the child was initially interpreted to prohibit in vitro fertilization of single mother or lesbian couples. This practice was, however, later changed due to the decisions of the Parliamentary Ombudsman that considered the practice as discriminatory.[149]

---

147. Tiitinen A: Sterilisaatio, Sterilisaatio – Terveyskirjasto, 11 Oct. 2022.
148. Salminen S, Burrell R, Lehtonen L: Hedelmöityshoidot, lisääntymisvapaus ja lapsen etu. Oikeustiede – Jurisprudentia 2007:XL, pp 303–404.
149. Yle: Naisparien ja itsellisten naisten hedelmöityshoidot käynnistyvät hiljalleen yliopistosairaaloissa – julkisella puolella hoidettiin aiemmin vain heteropareja, Naisparien ja itsellisten naisten

347. In vitro fertilization in Finland requires the written consent of the participants. The consent document must include the information to identify the person, the intended method of in vitro fertilization, any possible conditions for the treatment, the information on the expiration date of the consent and the clarification that the necessary information on the treatment and on the legal issues relating to IVF has been given to the participant. The participant and the representative of the service provider, who receives the consent, must sign the document. In the consent document, the donor of the gametes can put specific conditions for the use of his/her cells (e.g., exclude lesbian couples). The donor of sperm can in his consent document give permission that he can be declared to be the father of the child. This might be the case when IVF therapy is given to single mothers. According to section 3 of the Paternity Act (11/2015), however, the man giving consent to the IVF therapy of his spouse is usually considered to be the father of the child. If embryos of other persons are used in the in vitro fertilization, both the donor of the eggs and the donor of sperm must give their consent for their use.

348. According to section 11 of the Act, the donor of the gametes must be at least 18 years old and without hereditary or other diseases that could cause danger for the woman during the pregnancy or to the potential child. The data on the donor must be registered in the specific registry of the service provider and the child born based on the IVF therapy has according to section 23 of the Act the right to know the name of the donor when he/she turned 18 years old.

§4. Prenatal Diagnosis (Genetics in General)

349. Finland started a system of maternity clinics already in 1920s and by the late 1940s, the system covered all parts of the country. According to section 15 of the Healthcare Act, the counties are responsible for arranging these services to their inhabitants. The maternity clinics are widely used by pregnant women. An important incentive for the high coverage is that they give the certificate on pregnancy that grants the mother the right to financial maternity support of the special maternity package (which is chosen by most mothers in Finland).[150]

350. An important part of the work in maternity clinics is to follow the pregnancy and check the health of both mother and foetus. Every pregnant woman is entitled to two free ultrasound examinations, which usually are carried out around week 12 and week 20 of the pregnancy. In addition to the ultrasound, the foetal screening includes blood samples from the mother to analyse placental and foetal hormone and protein production to detect any anomalies. If there is suspicion on

hedelmöityshoidot käynnistyvät hiljalleen yliopistosairaaloissa – julkisella puolella hoidettiin aiemmin vain heteropareja (yle.fi); Lääkärilehti – Hedelmöityshoitojen mahdollisuudet (laakarilehti.fi), 11 Oct. 2022.

150. BBC: Why Finnish babies sleep in cardboard boxes, Why Finnish babies sleep in cardboard boxes – BBC News, 11 Oct. 2022.

malformation of the foetus, an amniocentesis may be performed in a hospital. The pregnant women are also screened for Human Immunodeficiency Virus (HIV) infection, syphilis, and hepatitis B.

351. As indicated in the Act on In Vitro Fertilization, it is forbidden to make selection of embryos based on their genetic profile in the process of IVF. However, exclusion of severe hereditary disease is allowed. As indicated in section 5 of the Act, the selection of the sex on an embryo is also forbidden in Finland, unless it is necessary to avoid a serious disease in the child.

352. The utilization of genetic data in healthcare has been discussed in Finland for several years.[151] In 2022, a proposition was made to establish a separate Genomic Centre that would develop the use of genetic data in research and healthcare. This Centre would be part of the functions of the National Supervisory Authority for Welfare and Health.[152]

§5. Psycho-Surgical Interventions

353. The general provision of following good medical practices as stated in section 15 of the Act on Healthcare Professionals applies also to psychiatry. This is separately stated in section 22b of the Mental Health Act (1116/1990). It stipulates that in the treatment of psychiatric disease only such involuntary procedures are allowed that are medically justifiable and whose omission would seriously endanger the health or safety of the patient of other persons.[153] Psycho-surgical interventions or other severe and irreversible intrusions are allowed only with the written consent of an adult patient if they are necessary to protect the life of the patient. However, electrical shock treatment is commonly used to treat severe depression and it can be given also against patient's will.

§6. Organ Transplants

354. The rules for organ transplantation in Finland are set in the Act on the Medical Use of Human Organs, Tissues, and Cells from 2001 (Tissue Act, 101/2001) that implemented the regulations of the EU Tissue Directive (Directive 2004/23/EC of the European Parliament and of the Council on setting standards of quality and safety for the donation, procurement, testing, processing, preservation, storage

151. Lehtonen, Lasse. Bio-oikeus lääketieteessä. Helsinki 2006.
152. Sosiaali-ja terveysministeriö: Hallituksen esitys Genomikeskuksen perustamiseksi eduskuntaan, Hallituksen esitys Genomikeskuksen perustamisesta eduskuntaan (valtioneuvosto.fi), 11 Oct. 2022.
153. Lobotomies were carried out in Finland, as in other European countries, in 1950s and early 1960s before the invention of modern antipsychotic drugs. Totally, some 1600 patients were operated. Herva R: Lobotomia oli oman aikansa tuote, Duodecim 2013:129,1499–1501, Lobotomia oli oman aikansa tuote (duodecimlehti.fi), 11 Oct. 2022.

and distribution of human tissues and cells). Transplantation of solid organs in Finland is centralized to Helsinki University Hospital, but organ and tissue procurement takes place around the whole country. In 2020, there were totally 263 renal, seventy-five liver and twenty-two heart transplantations in Helsinki University Hospital. Bone marrow transplantation is carried out in the haematological departments of all Finnish University Hospitals.

355. According to section 2 of the Act, the organs, tissues, or cells may be removed from a living donor who has given his/her consent to treat human disease or injury. Organs, tissues, or cells may, however, only be removed if this does not cause the donor any major health hazard or serious harm, if there is no treatment available for the recipient as effective as transplantation, and if no suitable organ, tissue, or cells from a dead donor are available, or the prognosis is expected to be appreciably better than the prognosis of transplantation from a deceased donor.

356. Adult persons able to decide about their treatment may donate non-regenerative organs or tissues only to treat disease or injury in a near relative or another person close to them. Under-age or incapacitated persons may only donate regenerative tissue or part of a regenerative organ to treat disease or injury threatening the life of a sibling if no suitable tissue or organ is available from a deceased or legally competent donor. A permit from the National Supervisory Authority for Welfare and Health is required for all removals of tissue or part of an organ from a living donor.

357. The removal of organs and tissues from a deceased donor is, however, rather liberal in Finland. Section 8 of the Tissue Act gives a general mandate to utilize organs, tissues, and cells from the deceased to be stored and used for later treatment of another person's disease or injury. The removal of organs from deceased donor is based on assumed consent. According to section 9 of the Act, organs, tissues, and cells of a deceased person may be removed unless it is known or there is reason to assume that the person would have objected while still alive. The deceased person's near relative or other close person must be given an explanation of the removal of organs, tissues or cells and of its significance. However, organs, tissues and cells of a deceased person may not be removed if this impedes investigation of the cause of death.

358. As required by the EU Tissue Directive, the Finnish Tissue Act prohibits the use of organs, tissues and cells, whose origin cannot be traced to treat human disease or injury. The healthcare unit or other unit storing human organs, tissues, and cells for the treatment of human disease or injury and using them for organ and tissue transplants has to keep a registry of the origin and use of the organs, tissues and cells to be able to trace both donors and recipients.

359. Section 18 of the Act prohibits the remuneration of organ and tissue donors and restricts the commercialization of human body parts. No donor or assignee of a representative of the donor may be promised or paid a fee for the removal and use of an organ, tissues, or cells or for the donation of a cadaver. Furthermore, it is prohibited to advertise for the need or availability of organs for the purpose of offering or seeking financial gain or comparable benefit. However, the donor of an organ, tissue or cells who suffers loss of income because of removal of an organ, tissue or cells is entitled to a daily allowance as provided in the Health Insurance Act (1224/2004). Not even the healthcare unit or other unit involved in removing, retaining, storing, or using organs, tissues and cells may pursue financial gain from the organ transplant activities. The healthcare unit or other tissue establishment may only charge handling fees for transporting organs, tissues, or cells, and for carrying out the tests needed to ensure safety and for providing storage. The charge made may not exceed the total cost of producing the service.

§7. Experiments on Human Beings

360. The ideologic background behind the modern regulation of medical research are in the Nürnberg principles and in the Declaration of Helsinki that are reflected in the Conventions of the Council of Europe. Finland joined the 1997 Convention on Human Rights in Biomedicine, even though the Convention was ratified only in 2009 after the Act on In Vitro Fertilizations was accepted in the parliament. However, the Act on Medical Research was accepted already in 1999. It sets the principles of medical research in Finland.[154] The general principles of the Act emphasize respect for human value. The Act requires that the wellbeing of the research subject is put superior to the interests of science and society. All risks and harms for the research subject should be prevented as much as possible.

361. Medical research is defined in section 2 of the Medical Research Act as research that involves intervention in the integrity of a person, human embryo, or human foetus for the purpose of increasing knowledge of health, the causes, symptoms, diagnosis, treatment and prevention of diseases or the nature of diseases in general. Intervention in the integrity could mean e.g., giving experimental medication or doing such extra procedures that are not part of the conventional therapy. Medical research also includes the research in health sciences. However, pure epidemiologic research that uses retrospective registry data does not fall under the Act on Medical Research. Also, psychologic experimentation as well as sports are outside the scope of the Act. However, the limits may be difficult to draw and the chosen methodology (i.e., if medical technology or data is used) affects also to the classification. In research the intent is, however, always to generate knowledge for scientific community, whereas e.g., in experimental therapy the main goal is to treat the patient.

362. Prior to the initiation of any research intervention, the investigator must evaluate the potential risks and harms for the research subjects. Those must be compared with the expected benefits for the patients or other subjects. The general

154. Lötjönen, Salla: Lääketieteellinen tutkimus ihmisillä. Oikeudellisia ja eettisiä näkökohtia ruumiilliseen koskemattomuuteen puuttumisesta lääketieteellisessä tutkimuksessa. Helsinki 2004.

requirements for medical research in Finland are listed in sections 3–5 of the Act. Firstly, section 3 requires that an independent research ethics board (IRB) has given a favourable opinion on the research protocol. If the research protocol is revised in substantial parts, the IRB must evaluate the change. There are regional IRBs in the five University Hospitals in Finland as well as one (TUKIJA) in the national level. Secondly, section 4 requires that the benefit and wellbeing of the research subject is placed above the interests of science and society. The investigator should try to prevent any predictable risk and harm to the research subject. He may be exposed only to such interventions that may produce greater health or scientific benefits than risks and harms. In addition to the investigator, also the IRB should take these into the consideration when giving its opinion. It should be emphasized that the research subject cannot give valid consent to research where this requirement is not fulfilled.

363. The third general requirement for medical research is according to section 4a of the Act that the investigator has adequate professional and scientific merits for that particular study. The study should have a medical doctor to look after the medical care of the research subjects. Furthermore, according to section 5 of the Act on the Medical Research, each study should have a sponsor. The investigator can also act as a sponsor.

364. According to section 6 of the Medical Research Act, medical research on a human subject is not allowed without the written consent of the subject. The requirement for written consent can, however, be overridden in emergencies or in cases where written consent is not possible due to the health status of the research subject. This exemption is not applied to clinical trials with pharmaceuticals, where written consent has to be obtained either from the research subject or from his/her representative.

365. To obtain a valid consent, the research subject should be given adequate information on his/her rights, on the purpose of the research, on the methods used as well as on the possible risks and harms. The information should be given in a way that the research subject is able to make his/her decision on participation with full knowledge on the issues affecting the consent. The consent can be withdrawn at any time.

366. The detailed content of the consent document is defined in the decree 986/1999 whose section 3 states that the consent document must include the following information:

- the name of the research subject, personal identification or birth date and address;
- clarification on the disclosure of information to the research subject and on the person who has disclosed it;
- information on the data sources where information on the research subject is collected;
- information to whom the research data is delivered and how the data protection is maintained;

- that the consent to research is voluntarily given; and
- information that the consent may be withdrawn without effect on possible medical therapy.

367. Both the research subject and the person obtaining the consent sign the document and a copy is given to the research subject.

368. The Medical Research Act restricts the possibilities to have an incapacitated person as a research subject. This is only possible if similar scientific results cannot be obtained with fully capacitated research subjects and if the study causes only little harm or stress to the research subject. The research should also produce direct benefits for the research subject himself or to the group of people he/she belongs. Furthermore, the incapacitated person can only act as a research subject if the legal representative has given consent for the research. If the incapacitated person objects any research activities, they cannot be performed.

369. A minor can according to section 18 of the Medical Research Act be a research subject only if the results of the research cannot be obtained with adult research subjects. The research may only pose minimal harm or stress for the minor. Furthermore, the research should bring direct benefits for the research subject or for the persons in the same age group or disease group. A minor of at least 15 years of age can give his/her consent to the research if he/she understands the purpose and impacts of the research. However, the guardian should also be notified on the participation. Otherwise, the consent of the guardian is required. If the minor under 15 years of age can understand the purpose and impacts of the research, also his/her consent is required for the research.

370. A pregnant or lactating woman can according to section 9 of the Medical Research Act be a research subject only, if similar results cannot be reached with other research subjects and the research will bring direct benefit for the health of the pregnant woman or her baby or to the health of her relatives or to other pregnant of lactating women or to foetus, newborn, or children of breastfeeding age.

371. A prisoner may act as a research subject only, if the research may bring direct health benefits to himself, to his/her relatives or to the health of other prisoners (Medical Research Act, section 10).

372. The research on human embryo and foetus is regulated in the Chapter 3 of the Act on Medical Research. Research with human embryos can be carried out only in institutions that have a specific permission for it. These permissions are granted by National Supervisory Authority for Welfare and Health (Valvira). The permissions are for institutions meaning that individual studies carried out in them do not need additional permission. However, they need a favourable statement from the regional ethics committee before the study can start. According to the Act on In Vitro Fertilizations the donors of eggs and sperm can give their permission that the extra embryos can be used in research.[155] The embryos cannot be used for research without the written consent of both donors (i.e., the donor of the eggs and the donor or sperm). They should receive adequate information on the purpose of the research. The donor can withdraw his/her consent by informing the research institution in question. The research in foetuses in the womb of the mother requires, however, only the consent of the mother. The research of foetus may be allowed e.g., when its purpose is to find cures for developmental disorders or congenital disease. The research on foetus should follow the general ethical principles of medical research. Therefore, the foetus may be disposed only to such interventions whose benefits clearly exceed the potential harms. The research may not endanger normal pregnancy.

373. According to Article 13 of the Biomedicine Convention, any intervention that aims to make changes to genome of a human being may be carried out only for a preventive, diagnostic and therapeutic purpose and only if the aim is not to change the hereditary characteristics of the offspring. Section 15 of the Act on Medical Research prohibits all research in human embryos and foetuses that aims to change the hereditary characteristics of the offspring unless the research aims to prevent or cure a severe hereditary disease. It should also be noted that the cloning of a human being is prohibited in section 4 of the Act on the Infertility Treatments (1237/2006).

§8. Euthanasia

374. Active euthanasia is not allowed in Finland. There was a citizen's initiative in 2017 in the Finnish parliament for allowing euthanasia made by two now former politicians.[156] The initiative emphasized that there should be more alternatives for end-of-life care for persons who experience intolerable suffering and pain. However, the Finnish parliament rejected the initiative for further legislative actions and instead suggested that there should be a multisectoral expert group to clarify the options for end-of-life care, which could then make suggestions for appropriate legislation.

375. The Finnish Medical Association opposes active euthanasia lining in its opinions with World Medical Association.[157]

376. Even though active euthanasia is not allowed in Finland, passive euthanasia (i.e., withholding a potentially life-saving treatment) is possible. Since section 6 of the Patient's Rights Act requires that the treatment is carried out in mutual understanding with the patient, the competent adult patient can refuse the treatment even though it would likely lead to the death of the patient.

---

155. Wallin, Laura: Alkio – ja kantasolututkimuksen sääntely bio-oikeudellisena mallina. Helsinki 2010.
156. Eduskunta: Eutanasia kansalaisaloite, Eutanasia-kansalaisaloite (eduskunta.fi), 11 Oct. 2022.
157. Lääkäriliitto: Lääkäriliiton kanta: hyvä saattohoito tärkeintä – ei eutanasialle, Lääkäriliitto – Lääkäriliiton kanta: hyvä saattohoito tärkeintä – ei eutanasialle (laakariliitto.fi), 11 Oct. 2022.

§9. Others (Transsexual Interventions)

377. The Act on Verification of the Gender of Transsexual Persons (563/2002) is currently under review.[158] The Act from 2002 requires for the formal change of sex that there is an adequate medical verification for the person belonging to the other gender than the biological identity displays and that the person wanting to change the legal sexual identity is a competent adult. Furthermore, the legal change of sex currently also requires that the person is not able to procreate.

378. The suggested proposition for the new legislation will abolish the requirement for infertility. The legal change of sexual identity will be based on the reliable verification that the person permanently feels belonging to the other gender. The change will require a cooling off period of thirty days prior to acceptance of the new gender in the Finnish identity registry. The medical professionals who have commented the proposition for the new Act have emphasized that the surgical operations should only be carried out after thorough psychiatric evaluation of the subject.

158. Sosiaali- ja terveysministeriö: Translaki, https://stm.fi/hanke?tunnus=STM009:00/2021, 11 Oct. 2022.

Part III. The Physician in Relation to the Healthcare System

Chapter 1. Collegial Relationships

§1. Associations

379. Out of the about 29,000 physicians in Finland (in 2021), some 28,000 belong to the Finnish Medical Association.[159] About 22,000 physicians are in their active working age. Medical students can also join the Finnish Medical Association. The membership fee includes also patient insurance for private practice. The Association arranges education (including the annual Doctor -event in Helsinki as well as the regional events) and negotiates the collective bargaining contracts with the employer's union. It also has supervising functions concerning the marketing of medical services as well as appropriate behaviour towards other physicians. In cases of inappropriate behaviour, the Association may issue a warning or even expel the member.

380. Medical doctors in Finland have many professional associations representing different medical specialties or scientific areas in medicine or biomedicine. They include the Finnish Society for Medical Law and Ethics (SLOES).[160]

381. Finnish nurses together with some other professional groups have a trade union The Union of Health and Social care Professionals in Finland (Tehy ry) that represents them in the negotiations for national collective bargaining contracts.[161] Of its 160,000 members, 20,000 are students. The unionization rate for nurses in the healthcare sector is over 90% making the union a powerful negotiator for nurse salaries.

159. Lääkäriliitto: The Finnish Medical Association, Lääkäriliitto – The Finnish Medical Association (laakariliitto.fi), 11 Oct. 2022.
160. Suomen Lääkintäoikeuden ja -etiikan Seura: Suomen Lääkintäoikeuden ja -etiikan Seura, Suomen Lääkintäoikeuden ja -etiikan Seura | sloes.fi, 11 Oct. 2022.
161. Tehy: We have the power to make a change, We have the power to make a change | Tehy, 11 Oct. 2022.

§2. Healthcare Centres

382. The services in the Finnish public healthcare are described in the Healthcare Act (1326/2010). The main objective of the Healthcare Act is to enhance customer orientation, to improve the quality and patient safety of healthcare, to promote health, to narrow regional health differences and to control the growth of healthcare expenses. In The Healthcare Act primary healthcare means public health services provided by local authorities, health promotion, and any related provision of health consulting and health checks, oral healthcare, medical rehabilitation, occupational healthcare, environmental healthcare, as well as emergency medical care, outpatient care, home nursing, at-home hospital care and inpatient care, mental health services, and substance abuse services where these are not covered by social services or specialized medical care.

383. Thus, healthcare services include medical examinations, which mean examination of illness. Healthcare services include also medical and dental diagnosis, treatment, and medicinal rehabilitation. Healthcare also includes the prevention of harms caused by illnesses that is to upholding health and ability to function, curing of illness, alleviating of and prevention of the worsening of symptoms and alleviating of suffering. Primary healthcare has the main responsibility of the treatment of a patient, but it can make an agreement with specialized medical care of partial responsibility for treatment of some diseases, for example, cancers. The distribution of work between primary healthcare and specialized medical care is based on a common agreement about a treatment of the totality of treatment. The emphasis of responsibility of treatment for example in the treatment of cancer can vary depending on the level the treatment requires. In addition, the early recognition of health issues and direction to treatment of a patient who need support, examinations and treatment are considered as healthcare services.

384. The Healthcare Act strongly emphasized equality. Section 10 of the Healthcare Act stipulates that the authorities organizing healthcare must ensure that healthcare services are available and universally accessible in the area to the residents that they are responsible for to provide services. The premise of providing healthcare services is the Uniform Grounds for Medical and Dental Care that the Ministry of Social Affairs and Health and National Institute for Welfare and Health have together drafted. The different authorities must together monitor how the uniform grounds are achieved in their operational field. However, the Healthcare Act is not applied on Åland Islands that organizes its healthcare in the limits of its self-government.

385. When coming into force in 2011, the Healthcare Act has significantly increased the freedom of choice in public healthcare. Since the beginning of 2014, patient has had the possibility to choose which ever health centre he/she wishes to as his/her treatment location for primary healthcare. Patient must make a written notification about which health centre he/she has chosen to both to the municipality which is in charge of his/her medical treatment and to the chosen municipality's health centre. The responsibility about the treatment of the patient in question is transferred to the chosen municipality's health centre not later than after three weeks the notification has arrived. Patient can choose only one health centre at the time. Patient can make a new choice earliest after a year has passed from the previous choice.

386. The Healthcare Act includes a special provision about the medical services of students. A student, who must reside in other region than that of his/her place of –domicile due to his/her studies, can receive treatment in the hospital or other healthcare unit of the region where he/she is studying. The same applies to a person who must reside in another place then his/her place of domicile due to work. In addition, if there is another factor which requires that the person must necessarily be treated in another region than his/her place of domicile, this provision can also be taken into consideration.

387. The freedom to choose specialized medical care services is restricted by an examination made to estimate the need for such services, both in medicine and in dentistry. If a physician or a dentist estimates that a person needs services from specialized medical care, patient can choose the public hospital within Finland where he/she wishes to receive the treatment. The treatment location must be chosen in a consensus with the physician or dentist issuing the referral.

388. Primary healthcare from 2023 onwards is organized by wellbeing service counties. The services are provided at public health centres. Every municipality has still in 2022 legal obligation to have a health centre (or a wellbeing centre in the future according to the terminology of the new social and healthcare legislation) either alone or together with other municipalities. This obligation is transferred to counties in 2023. Before the corona epidemic in 2019, there were totally 22.8 million patient visits in public primary healthcare. Of these were 5.9 million appointments to the doctor indicating that most visits were handled by nurses and other healthcare professionals. Totally 3.7 million people i.e., 67% of the Finnish population used the services of health centres in 2019.[162]

389. The healthcare centres in Finland are public authorities that have multiple tasks according to the Finnish legislations. The physicians working in health centres are public officials in their status. This means that their appointment takes place following the rules of public law and that they bear similar legal responsibilities as other public officials for possible mistakes in office.

390. According to section 48 of the Healthcare Act (1326/2010), a person can choose the care centre where he/she wants to be treated by making a written notice to the municipality/county in charge of the centre. However, a new change in healthcare centre can be made only after one year. The patient has also the possibility to select the physician or other healthcare professional that is treating him/her in the

---

162. THL: Perusterveydenhuollon ja suun terveydenhuollon avohoitokäynnit 2019, Tilastoraportti 30/2020, https://www.julkari.fi/bitstream/handle/10024/140239/TR_30_2020.pdf?sequence=5&isAllowed=y, 11 Oct. 2022.

limits of feasible arrangement of the services. If feasible, the patient should be directed to the physician or other healthcare professional that has been treating him/her previously. However, due to lack or high turnover of personnel in health centres, the selection of physician is often not possible in practice if the patient wants to have the appointment with a short notice.

391. The continuation of treatment in Finland is ensured with access to electronic health records. It is obligatory for physicians in most cases to make their notes to the electronic health record system that is connected to the national patient data repository.[163] The physicians and other healthcare professionals treating the patient has access to this data with their individual identification codes. The patient has also the possibility to block the access and check, who have been looking his/her patient records.

392. Some health centres have tried to establish teams of professionals that include physicians, nurses, physiotherapists, and social workers. However, usually physicians in health centres work with a receptionist and/or assisting nurse. Nurses also work rather independently with patients with stable chronic diseases like diabetes or asthma. Nowadays the physicians in healthcare centres work only daytime, since the 24/7 emergency services in Finland are concentrated into hospitals that also employ acute medicine physicians or general practitioners to take care of the acute patients.

393. Especially for junior physicians working in health centre, the adequate guidance to the practical work of a primary care physician is of great importance. Those units that have good reputation for education can recruit physicians much more easily than those units, where appropriate work guidance is lacking.

394. Health centre's responsibility also includes distribution of equipment required to provide treatment at home. Providing rehabilitating equipment is part of the treatment and need for them must be made clear in patient's treatment plan. In the treatment of some chronic diseases, some materials and devices are distributed to patients without compensation as their individual needs require. Such materials are for example blood regulation strips for diabetics, strips for examination of urine, syringes of insulin, insulin pens and insulin needles and lancets required for taking of blood samples and a terminable lending of blood sugar indicators.

§3. Professional Duties Toward Colleagues

395. There is no legislation on collegial relationships between physicians in Finland. The Finnish Medical Association has, however, published guidelines concerning collegial relationships between physicians.[164] The instructions ask physicians to

163. Kanta: Patient data repository, Patient Data Repository – Professionals – Kanta.fi, 15 Oct. 2022.
164. Lääkäriliitto: Kollegiaalisuusohjeet, Lääkäriliitto – Kollegiaalisuusohjeet (laakariliitto.fi), 15 Oct. 2022.

act collegially and with dignity as well as to follow good manners among medical professionals. Good co-operation between physicians works for the benefit of the patients. The guidelines apply to all activities where physicians interact including the public activities and social media. They also apply when making patient records or giving medical certificates and answering consultations. If there are discrepancies in professional opinion concerning between physicians, they should be solved with direct negotiations between the physicians.

396. If the patient is transferred to another healthcare unit, the treating physicians should give all necessary information noting, however, the data protection regulation, for the good treatment of the patient.

397. If the disputes between physician cannot be solved in negotiations, they can be submitted to the Finnish Medical Association for a settlement.

Chapter 2. Relationship with Other Healthcare Providers

§1. Pharmacists

398. Pharmacists are one group of the healthcare professionals that are mentioned in section 5 of the Act on Healthcare Professionals (262/2015). Physicians, dentists and to certain degree nurses (with specific training) have the right to prescribe drugs in Finland. Their delivery takes place from the pharmacies that in Finland are owned by individual pharmacists. Pharmacists in Finland rarely work in health centres, but their number in hospitals has been increasing in the last few years. Hospital pharmacists, in addition of distributing drugs, now take part in the checking of the medication lists of the patients and educating them on the proper use of their medicines.

399. The Finnish pharmacy system is peculiar, still having features that were common in Scandinavia in the nineteenth century. Under section 40 of the Medicines Act (395/1987), the operation of a pharmacy business requires a license (pharmacy license) issued by the Finnish Medicines Agency (FIMEA).[165] A pharmacy license can only be granted to a licensed pharmacist. The other requirements are that he/she has not been declared bankrupt, has not been assigned a guardian, has not been restricted in their functional capacity and has not a criminal record of an offence thought to affect pharmacy operations. If there is more than one applicant, a pharmacy license is granted to the applicant who can be considered to overall has the best potential for operating a pharmacy business. In assessing the potential, the applicant's work in pharmacies and other pharmaceutical services and studies, managerial skills and other activities pertinent to operating a pharmacy business must be taken into account.

400. In 2020 there were totally 627 pharmacies in Finland operating in 819 locations (some pharmacies also have branch offices). The system of granting license to hold a pharmacy is based on the idea that without specific requirements for the location of the premises, all pharmacies would concentrate on cities leaving a large part of the country without drug supplies.[166] However, there is also a lot of lobbying from the association of pharmacies keeping the business restricted. The Finnish competition authorities have several times pointed out that the restrictions in competition increase drug prices in Finland.[167]

401. According to section 56 of the Medicines Act, each pharmacy must have adequate number of staff that have a pharmacy degree. They should also regularly participate to in-service training to keep up their competence.

---

165. Fimea: Pharmacy licences, Pharmacy licences – fimea englanti – Fimea, 15 Oct. 2022.
166. Nyblin, Klaus: Lääkelainsäädännön käsikirja. Helsinki 2018.
167. Finnish Competition and Consumer Authority: The FCCA pharmacy market study proposes measures to reduce the costs of medicines for consumers and society, The FCCA pharmacy market study proposes measures to reduce the costs of medicines for consumers and society – Finnish Competition and Consumer Authority (kkv.fi), 15 Oct. 2022.

§2. Nurses (Midwives)

402. Section 22 of the Act on Healthcare Professionals (559/1994) stipulates that the licensed physician decides on diagnosis and treatment of medical patients and the licensed dentist on diagnosis and the treatment of dental patients. This rule has in Finish legal practice meant that physicians, as well as dentists for their part, are also in a supervisory role for other healthcare professionals. They should be able to check that the treatment, even when realized by other professionals, follows their instructions and good medical practice. This obligation to supervise other healthcare professional is also shown in the Finnish court praxis.[168]

403. Nurses in Finland go through a long education and they can take tasks from doctors. This is also made possible by section 2 of the Act on the Healthcare Professionals which stipulates that healthcare professionals can work in the tasks of other healthcare professionals, if they have adequate education, experience, and competence for it. The transfer of tasks, however, has to be based on feasible production of healthcare services as well as for appropriate arrangements in the workplace. The National Supervisory Authority for Welfare and Health (Valvira) interprets this to require both adequate workplace education for the person, as well as written instructions on the tasks and responsibilities of each professional. A typical example for this is the role of midwives in deliveries, which they often handle without the presence of a physician. There may be problems, however, if there are no appropriate instructions available in the maternity hospital, when the obstetrician must be called.

404. Even though the physician has supervisory responsibilities for the treatment, some authors of legal research think that the real legal responsibility would require clear mention in the contract of employment on this supervisory position.[169] However, the court cases have also emphasized the role of professional training of physicians and nurses, and state that a physician who is not correcting the dangerous or erroneous practices of nurses is also liable for the possible damages that the actions of the nurses may cause.

405. In practice, the transfer of tasks from physicians to nurses has often obstacles due to trade union policies. The trade union activists of nurses tend to ask higher salaries for any new responsibilities and quite often the hospitals lack the funds for it.

406. Nursing at home is defined as a healthcare provided outside healthcare unit. Healthcare professionals in charge of home nursing or home hospital operations can provide treatment at the home of the patient. Patient's need for treatment must be evaluated in a defined healthcare unit, where a treatment plan is drafted and where

168. Finnish Supreme Court 1988:34, KKO:1988:34–Korkeimman oikeuden ennakkopäätökset – FINLEX ® and 1979 II 69, KKO:1979-II-69–Korkeimman oikeuden ennakkopäätökset – FINLEX ®, 15 Oct. 2022.
169. Nuutila, Ari-Matti: Rikosoikeudellinen huolimattomuus. Jyväskylä 1996.

a patient receives referral to home nursing or home hospital. A healthcare unit is in charge of necessary treatment related examinations. A patient receiving treatment at home must have possibility to be in contact with healthcare unit, if needed.

§3. PARAMEDICAL PROFESSIONALS

407. Emergency services (prehospital care and ambulances) in Finland are mostly handled by rescue departments (Pelastuslaitos), whose staff includes not only firemen but also paramedics. Medical support for them is organized by hospitals, whose emergency rooms offer consultation for the ambulances in field. There are some private ambulances in Finland as well, but they mostly take care of patient transfers and not emergency care. The emergency number in Finland 112 connects the caller to the National Emergency Response Centre Agency that allocates the tasks to regional rescue services with minimal delays.[170] The Emergency Response Centre Agency operates under the Ministry of the Interior. The Agency has a statutory mandate to answer emergency calls, evaluate their urgency and forward any calls that require immediate action to rescue services, the police, social services or health authorities. From the beginning of 2023, fire brigades and emergency departments are organizationally a part of the welfare regions and have a common financing from the state budget.

408. In addition to ambulances, there are also helicopters available for medical rescue operations. These are operated by the state-owned FinHEMS company together with the university hospitals from eight helicopter bases around Finland.[171] They had some 14,000 emergency calls in 2020.

409. The requirements for emergency units in Finland are stated in the Governmental Decree 585/2017. Typically, the first response unit in an accident is a fire truck. Their personnel are trained to assess the vital status of the patient and start resuscitation before an ambulance arrives. However, the first response units are not participating into the transfer of the patient.

410. The baseline first response units are ambulances that mostly perform patients transfers of stable patients. Their staff consists of two paramedics, one of which must have a training of a healthcare professional (as stipulated in the Act on Healthcare Professionals).

411. The treatment level first response units have the capabilities necessary for treating acute patients. Their staff consists of two persons, of which one has to be nurse or specifically trained paramedic and the other to be a paramedic with baseline response unit competence.

---

170. Emergency Response Centre Agency: Stay safe, Emergency Response Centre Agency – Emergency Response Centre Agency – Finland (112.fi), 15 Oct. 2022.
171. FinnHeRMS: Lääkärihelikopteripalvelua Suomessa, FinnHEMS – FinnHEMS, 15 Oct. 2022.

412. The first response units operate under the directions of a specific field manager that usually works in the hospital emergency department and coordinates the activity on ambulances. There are also first response units (like helicopters) that have a physician in their staff.[172]

413. The tasks of the field manager include participation to the first response tasks, direct the use of first response units and ambulances in the area and to support the Emergency response agency in cases, where there is a need to deviate on routine activities and instructions e.g., when there is a high load of first response tasks.

414. The hospital districts/counties are responsible for making the decisions on service levels for emergency services. The decisions include the requirements for the response times for ambulance arrivals in different parts of Finland.[173] According to section 38 of the Healthcare Act the service level decision shall also include the organization of emergency services, the type of services, the competence requirements of the staff and other necessary aspects of emergency services in the area. Emergency care must be planned and produced in co-operation with healthcare units so that together they will form a regionally functional unity.[174] The welfare county must run the operative actions of the emergency care and draft guidance for directing patients needing transportations to treatment and guidance for situations where patient doesn't require transportation. Furthermore, the region must draft guidance for alert instructions and other instructions for emergency services, which the regional emergency care unit will make compatible with the instructions given by the National Emergency Response Centre.

415. The emergency care centre of co-operation area around a university hospital has to adapt the emergency centre services of the regions in its field of operation, and give guidance to them with consideration for regional special characteristics like language and geographical circumstances. Furthermore, they have to prepare with other emergency care centres of other special responsibility areas and adapt a national guidance for emergency care operations. In addition, emergency care service must match together the electronic patient information systems used in the emergency services in its area and also match other information systems the hospital districts used, so that together they form a functioning unity as agreed with the regions.

---

172. Sosiaali- ja terveysministeriö: Ensihoito, Ensihoito – Sosiaali- ja terveysministeriö (stm.fi), 15 Oct. 2022.
173. Valtioneuvosto: Ohje ensihoitopalvelujen palvelutasopäätöksen laatimiseksi, Ohje ensihoitopalvelujen palvelutasopäätöksen laatimiseksi – Valto (valtioneuvosto.fi), 15 Oct. 2022.
174. The Ministry of Social Affairs and Health has given a decree on organizing emergency care 340/2011.

Chapter 3. Relationship with Healthcare Institutions

§1. Hospitals

416. The hospital system in Finland has evolved from the state-owned hospitals to regional hospitals that are run by municipalities of their co-operative unions. From the beginning of 2023 onwards, the municipality owned units will be replaced by wellbeing service counties that are funded by the state. The aim is to integrate the hospitals with primary care and social care.

417. General hospitals in Finland are classified into three levels: university hospitals, central hospitals and regional hospitals. In addition, there are several psychiatric hospitals. In 2020 there are totally five university hospitals and sixteen central hospitals in Finland. There are over thirty regional hospitals in Finland, some of which are operated by a city as a part of the health centre functions. Most psychiatric hospitals are nowadays part of the university hospitals or central hospitals. However, the city of Helsinki is still running its own psychiatric hospital. Furthermore, there are two psychiatric state hospitals that take care of patients that have committed serious crimes but have been found insane.

418. Finnish hospitals in 2019 had 9,8 million patient visits.[175] They have over 18,000 hospital beds for the patients.[176] Furthermore, the health centres have additional 6,500 beds for their patients.

419. About half of the Finnish physicians of working age, work in hospitals. They are appointed as public officers and have some key responsibilities for the function of the public healthcare system in Finland (including emergency service and crisis management). In 2020–2021 the medical leadership of university hospitals had an important role in the evaluation of measures that were needed to contain the COVID-19 epidemic.[177]

420. There is not a clear definition of a hospital in the Finnish legislation. However, hospitals as institutions are characterized for having beds for overnight healthcare services and are lead/supervised by physicians (unlike nursing homes). The Finnish hospitals, as hospitals in most other countries, must have a chief medical officer to supervise the diagnosis and treatment of patients as stipulated in section 57 of the Healthcare Act. The hospital managers, instead, don't have to be healthcare professionals at all.

175. Kuntaliitto: Sairaanhoitopiirien tammi–joulukuu 2020. Sairaanhoitopiirien tammi–joulukuu 2020 | Kuntaliitto.fi, 15 Oct. 2022.
176. Valtioneuvosto: Selvitys sairaansijojen määrästä ja alueellisesta jakautumisesta Suomessa, https://julkaisut.valtioneuvosto.fi/bitstream/handle/10024/162580/STM_2020_36_rap.pdf, 15 Oct. 2022.
177. HUS: Koronavirustilanne, rajoitukset ja suositukset, Koronavirusepidemiatilanne, rajoitukset ja suositukset | HUS, 15 Oct. 2022.

421. Even though section 24 of the Healthcare Act stipulates that municipalities/ wellbeing service counties are responsible on the treatment of diseases; the Act doesn't mention general hospitals at all. Instead, it mentions the services of specialized healthcare (meaning the services of former hospital districts). Section 42 of the Healthcare Act states, however, that the hospital districts/counties that have a university hospital in their area must organize the most demanding specialized healthcare for the whole responsibility area. At the moment, the new welfare regions are planning their activities, as well as the practical co-operation of the hospitals with both primary healthcare and social care.

§2. Preventive Healthcare

422. Finland has been a front-runner in some areas of preventive healthcare. The maternity clinics were established some 100 years ago in the 1920s. The health of children has after that improved remarkably. Finland has also been able to reduce significantly cardiovascular mortality during the past 50 years. The North Karelia Project that focused to the reduction of cardiovascular risk factors in the population of Eastern Finland was a great success and has been an example for many other countries.[178]

423. Section 19 paragraph 3 of the Finnish Constitution stipulates that the public authorities must promote the health of the population. The obligation of public authorities to promote health refers to both the preventive actions in health and social care and to develop the circumstances of the society to a direction which would promote health. According to the Government Proposal 9/2010 for the Healthcare Act, the obligation includes that the services secured in the Act are provided with high-quality to the residents of the municipality.

424. Chapters 2 and 3 of the Healthcare Act contain provisions about the contents of primary healthcare services. As a preventive service, the region has to organize health information distribution and physical health examinations, screenings, prenatal clinics and child welfare clinics, school healthcare, occupational healthcare, mariner healthcare, the consulting services for older persons, environmental healthcare, and to ensure that residents or patients have possibility to obtain the necessary medical certificates. The county must also ensure that the necessary medical care (which includes primary healthcare, home nursing, oral healthcare, mental health services, substance abuse services, medical rehabilitation, other forms of rehabilitation and executive assistance) are organized properly. It is important to note that since the Act emphasizes the equality of services, the region that is providing services doesn't have a lot of discretion to choose for example the emphasis on health promotion.

---

178. The National Institute for Health and Welfare: The North-Karelia Project fundamentally changed the lifestyle of Finns and increased healthy years of live, The North Karelia Project fundamentally changed the lifestyle of Finns and increased healthy years of life – News – THL, 15 Oct. 2022.

425. Section 3 of the Healthcare Act defines health promotion as actions aimed at individuals, population, communities, and living environments with a view of maintaining and improving health, work ability and functional capacity, influencing determinants of health, preventing illnesses, accident injuries, and other health problems, strengthening mental health, and reducing health inequalities between different population groups, as well as systematic targeting of resources in a manner that promotes better public health. The definition is quite wide.

426. Section 11 of the Healthcare Act includes a duty to take health and welfare aspects into consideration in all operations. Decisions about health and welfare are made and executed, in addition to social and health services, on all fields, including planning and construction, executing of housing, traffic planning and education and work. Exercise, youth and culture services can also significantly promote health and welfare. The effects of decisions may be different on different population groups. Preliminary estimate of social and health effects can help to estimate the effects on different population groups as a part of normal preparation work. The aim is to bring more openly health promotion into the public decision making. Section 12 of the Healthcare Act obliges the counties to promote health and welfare. The main objective of social and health policies is to promote health and social wellbeing and to prevent health problems.

427. The municipalities are required to make a plan for health promotion in each term of the city council. According to section 6 of the Act on Organization of Social and Healthcare Services (621/2021), the municipalities must promote the wellbeing and health of their inhabitants. They should set goals and define actions in their strategic planning. Furthermore, before municipalities are making decisions, they should make an evaluation on the impact of the decision to the wellbeing and health in different sociodemographic groups. They should also appoint the responsible party to promote wellbeing and health, follow the living conditions, wellbeing and health in different areas and groups. The results should be reported annually to the city council. The municipalities should make a report on the findings to the counties and make the report available for the public. The municipalities must co-operate with other public bodies and private organizations to promote wellbeing and health.

428. Section 7 of the Act on the Organization of Social and Healthcare services stipulates that the counties have the primary responsibility on health promotion, when it is linked to the other responsibilities of the region. The counties must in their strategic planning set goals and define actions for the promotion of wellbeing and health. They must also evaluate the impact of their decisions on the wellbeing and health of the different sociodemographic groups. The counties must appoint a responsible party for the tasks of promoting wellbeing and health. They must also follow the living conditions, wellbeing and health in different areas and groups. The counties must in co-operation with the municipalities, make a regional report and plan on the wellbeing of their people. The report and plan must be publicly available.

429. The municipalities will get some funding from the state for their activities as stipulated in section 15 of the Act 618/2021. The amount of the funding will dependent on the indicators that describe the wellbeing of the inhabitants.

430. Mental health work is defined as the promotion of the mental wellbeing, ability to cope and personal growth of the individual, and the prevention, curing and alleviation of mental illness and other mental disorders. This definition on mental health work is included into section 1 of the Mental Health Act (1116/1990).

431. The objectives of mental health work are good mental health of population meaning population's good ability to function and safety. Mental health work includes mental health services provided for people suffering from mental disturbances in order to support and heal the mental health disturbance, alleviate its symptoms and help people with such illnesses to maintain or return their ability to function. Treatment and rehabilitation served as mental health services must be based on medical examination and must follow good treatment and rehabilitation practices. Mental health services must be customer orientated and based on individual requirements. The possibility to seek treatment must be supported, especially since people with mental disturbances are easily stigmatized and their ability to take care of themselves can possibly be decreased.

§3. Health Insurance

432. Finland has utilized both Beveridge-type system of health services and Bismarck type of health insurance in organizing the healthcare services. The national health insurance covers medical expenses from private healthcare. It doesn't compensate the user fees of public healthcare. The costs must be necessary for the treatment of disease of pregnancy and the compensated treatment must follow good medical practice. Currently, the compensation for medical expenses via the insurance system is low, since the nominal prices do not correspond the real-life price level.[179] However, dental expenses are more adequately covered (60% from the nominal price) by the National Health Insurance system. The insurance compensation is in most cases applied by the service provider that charges from the patient just the part of the fee that is not compensated from the insurance.

433. The private medical services were initially in the 1960s heavily supported by the National Health Insurance. However, after the economic depression in the early 1990s in Finland, the occupational healthcare that is organized by the employers got a more important role. Due to problems to access the primary care, employers started to organize healthcare for their employees. Most working age Finns nowadays use the occupational health service as their primary healthcare. The National Social Insurance (Kela) also reimburses employers for a share of the costs for occupational healthcare in each accounting period. Organization and funding of

179. Kela: Sairaanhoitokorvausten taksat, sairaanhoitokorvausten-taksaluettelo-1-7-2022-alkaen.pdf | Kela, 15 Oct. 2022.

occupational healthcare is part of labour market politics meaning that the premises are agreed in three-party negotiations between trade unions, employers' organizations and the government.

434. Since the role of the National Health Insurance has diminished during the past years and their level on reimbursement on private fees decreased (reimbursements rates for doctor's fees are in real life just 5% or less on the official acceptable rates which also are much below the actual fees), the private health insurance has taken a bigger role in compensating healthcare costs. This is seen especially in children, since parents very often take a health insurance for their kids to get better access to primary care and even to specialists. In 2020 some 45% of children in Finland had a private insurance for healthcare costs.

435. The National Health Insurance is very important in compensating the expenses of pharmacotherapy.[180] In Finland, pharmaceuticals are classified to three different categories, whose costs are covered with different compensation levels. In the basic category the compensation level is 40% of the price of the drug. In the lower special category, the compensation level is 65% of the price of the drug. In the upper special category, the compensation level is 100%, but there is a personal responsibility of EURs 4,5 for each drug. If the amount annual personal responsibility exceeds EUR 592.16 the overriding part is compensated. However, the patient must thereafter cover EUR 2.5 for each purchased drug.[181]

§4. Others (Occupational Healthcare)

436. An occupational healthcare professional is defined in the Act on Healthcare Professionals as a healthcare professional, who has the competence of specialized physician in occupational health or other licensed physician or public health nurse who has the required education to operate on occupational health services. Occupational healthcare professionals are physicians and public health nurses who on the base of their education have the competence to determine the connections between work and health and thus possibility to work as healthcare professionals in charge of occupational healthcare services. Government decree 1484/2001 includes more precise provisions for the education of occupational healthcare professionals. The Decree also includes provisions about the principles of good quality occupational healthcare services and of the contents of occupational healthcare services.[182]

437. Section 3 of the Act on Occupational Healthcare defines an expert of occupational healthcare services. Expert of occupational healthcare is defined as a person who has either the competence of physiotherapist or psychologist and has

180. Arajärvi, Pertti: Johdatus sosiaalioikeuteen. Helsinki 2011.
181. Kela: Lääkekorvaukset, Lääkekorvaukset – kela.fi, 15 Oct. 2022.
182. Finlex: Valtioneuvoston asetus hyvän työterveyshuoltokäytännön periaatteista, työterveyshuollon sisällöstä sekä ammattihenkilöiden ja asiantuntijoiden koulutuksesta, 708/2013–Säädösmuutosten hakemisto–FINLEX ®, 15 Oct. 2022.

sufficient information on occupational healthcare or he/she has education on work-hygiene, ergonomics or on technic or similar field and has sufficient knowledge about occupational health or has other specialized medical degrees than that of occupational health. Occupational healthcare professionals and experts must be professionally independent from the employer, employees and of their representatives. If the employer organizes occupational healthcare services as its own operations, the employer cannot within his management direct the occupational healthcare professionals, when it is a question of the contents of occupational healthcare services (such as when one is ordered to treatment).

438. Employer or entrepreneur can organize other healthcare services in addition to occupational healthcare services. If they decide to do so, a written agreement must be made with the occupational healthcare services provided as stipulated in section 14 of the Occupational Healthcare Act. Even though the employer is in charge of organizing occupational healthcare services, employer must work in co-operation with employees and occupational healthcare services provided as stipulated in section 8 of the Occupational Healthcare Act (so-called principle of co-operation). Before the employer decides how the occupational healthcare services are to be organized or decides about another important fact affecting the occupational healthcare services, the matter must be handled in work safety committee as stipulated in the Act on Supervision of Occupational Safety and Appeal in Occupational Safety Matters or on co-operation procedure replacing such a committee.

439. In practice, the principle of co-operation means that employees and their representatives have possibility to make suggestions to develop occupational healthcare services and receive expert help to determine how much the work strains them or how much does it affect the health of employees.

Selected Bibliography

Arajärvi, Pertti: Johdatus sosiaalioikeuteen. Helsinki 2011.

Burrell, Riitta: Naisia ja sikiöitä. Helsinki 2003.

Lahti, Raimo: Lääkintäoikeus – kehittyvä uusi tieteenala. Lakimies 1997:6, 753–759.

Lehtonen, Lasse: Potilaan yksityisyyden suoja. Suomalainen Lakimiesyhdistys 2001.

Lehtonen, Lasse. Bio-oikeus lääketieteessä. Helsinki 2006.

Lehtonen L, Lohiniva-Kerkeä M, Pahlman I: Terveysoikeus. Helsinki 2015.

Lötjönen, Salla: Lääketieteellinen tutkimus ihmisillä. Oikeudellisia ja eettisiä näkökohtia ruumiilliseen koskemattomuuteen puuttumisesta lääketieteellisessä tutkimuksessa. Helsinki 2004.

Mäenpää, Olli: Hallinto-oikeus. Helsinki 2013.

Niemivuo, Matti: Uusi aluehallinto – hyvinvointialueista maakuntaitsehallintoon? Kauppakamari 2022.

Nordic Legal Research Group on Health Law: Patient's consent to treatment – a nordic perspective on medical self-determination, Nordic_LRG_Medical_Law.pdf (elsa.org), 16 October 2022.

Nyblin, Klaus: Lääkelainsäädännön käsikirja. Helsinki 2018.

Pahlman, Ilma: Potilaan itsemääräämisoikeus. Helsinki 2006.

Salminen S, Burrell R, Lehtonen L: Hedelmöityshoidot, lisääntymisvapaus ja lapsen etu. Oikeustiede – Jurisprudentia 2007:XL, sections 303–404.

Tuori K, Kotkas T: Sosiaalioikeus. Helsinki 2016.

Wallin, Laura: Alkio- ja kantasolututkimuksen sääntely bio-oikeudellisena mallina. Helsinki 2010.

Selected Bibliography

Index

The numbers here refer to paragraph numbers

Index

Index

www.ingramcontent.com/pod-product-compliance
Lightning Source LLC
Chambersburg PA
CBHW071350230926
51846CB00002B/493